Treasury of American Gardens

TREASURY OF

American Gardens

James M. Fitch & F. F. Rockwell

HARPER & BROTHERS | NEW YORK

Acknowledgments

The publishers wish to thank the Garden Club of America for its cooperation in the course of the selection of gardens represented in the book.

They are also pleased to be able to thank Mr. John Brimer for his advice and work in the preparation of ground plans and planting diagrams.

Prepared and produced by Chanticleer Press, Inc., New York

Contents

PACIFIC COAST AND HAWAII

FROM WESTERN DESERT TO SOUTHERN SWAMP GARDENS

SPECIAL FORMS

Preface

THE PURPOSE of this book is twofold. First, it is designed to present to the reader a panorama of American gardens, old and modern, large and small, which will show how gardening in the United States had its beginnings, what shaped those beginnings, and the changes that have taken place up to the present.

Secondly, a survey of these gardens should provide a great many useful suggestions to those interested in creating gardens of their own. Any individual garden, like the development of any plant, must be a matter of growth—growth, above all, within the mind of the gardener through the accumulation of ideas from many sources and the assimilation of these ideas into a plan for a harmonious whole.

In deciding which gardens were to be represented in this collection, we have not selected only those that appealed to us personally. We have sought, rather, to give the reader a panoramic view of what has happened and is happening in the landscaping of the American home, and why. Considering the vastness of the subject, we could hope only to sample the countless styles and traditions in use today. We have tried to consider all available material; if we have not always succeeded, it was not for lack of effort.

It may be pointed out that in the great majority of the gardens shown in this book, there is one overriding characteristic: *they are in harmony with the houses which they surround.* Both architecturally and esthetically the residence and its grounds should be in accord if the resultant whole is to be good. For the most part, too, both house and garden in any particular region fit into the general physical and cultural atmosphere of that region. It is not without cause that the small, trim and picket-bound gardens of New England, tended for the most part by the loving hands of their owners, differed so greatly from the elaborately planned acres of Virginia plantations, with endless clipped boxwood hedges kept in condition by innumerable slaves.

The presentation in this book is organized—insofar as was practical—according to geographic regions. In general these regions have determined the plant material used in each garden. In the earlier days, too, existing economic and social conditions in these several regions influenced, no less than the climate, the types of gardens constructed. The book, then, unfolds a sort of grand circle tour of American gardens, starting with the colonial plantations of the Middle South, going northward through Pennsylvania and New York to New England, across country through the Midwest to the Northwest, down the Pacific coast to California, eastward through the central desert area to the Gulf coast, and back to the old Deep South. This is a generous-sized canvas, and no effort was made to follow a rigid sequence or to represent an area merely for the sake of representation.

This brings us to a final consideration. One cannot help noting, as the gradual changes from early to present-day American gardens are observed, that whereas the former were designed primarily to walk in—or through—those of today are being designed to *live* in. It is becoming more and more difficult, in terms of design, to tell just where the house stops and the garden begins. With modern glass walls taking the place of old-fashioned windows, the garden becomes part of the interior of the home—and must be planned accordingly. This is the real revolution in American gardening that is going on today.

JAMES M. FITCH
FREDERICK FRYE ROCKWELL

7

American Gardens from the Beginning

AMERICA is a land of changes. In the beginning, along the eastern coast from the Canadian border down to Florida these changes were slow, and sectional. As the tide of colonization swept westward, the tempo of change increased, but it still remained sectional. If one traveled from the East to the West or from the North to the South, it was not merely the terrain and the temperature which altered, but also the whole economic and social structure, including the way it expressed itself in architecture and landscape design.

With the development of ever more rapid methods of communication and transportation, these sectional differences grew less and less. And with the growth of magazines and newspapers with nation-wide circulations in the multimillions, setting the patterns for how people will live, the homes they will build, and the gardens they will create, the old differences have diminished almost to the vanishing point. In fact, today a person arriving by plane in almost any city—or even in any large town—seeing the same red and green flashing neon signs, the same window displays, and even the same store names as those he might happen to be familiar with two or three thousand miles away, might readily believe that he had been flown in a circle back to the place from which he had started.

All this, of course, has had its effect upon gardening as well as upon architecture—for the two are inseparably bound together. Today the New England or Southern or California gardens which could be called typical are few indeed. Such gardens of course still have their own characteristic plant material—just as the houses vary to some extent in the materials of which they are constructed—but in their basic, functional design all of them have been blended. Gardens have become, like our American dwellings, something new, existing in their own right.

The American garden of today is unlike any other in the world. And yet it has certain qualities in common with all the great garden traditions of the world: Chinese and Japanese, Arabic, Persian, English,

French and Italian. Its international origin is, in fact, what makes the American garden unique. Unlike the traditional garden of all the older countries, it has been swept over by tide after tide of foreign influence. It bears the evidences of these cultural inundations. Unlike the Persian or the Chinese, for example—which through the accident of isolation were able to flourish without change for centuries—the American garden has never in its three centuries of cultivation been cut off from the stimulation of new forms and new plant materials. These it has adopted eagerly—too eagerly some would say; but, for better or for worse, these have become part of its very essence.

This stimulation from outside has given American gardens their multiform variety—this and the fact that they have been built in climates which duplicate all the major climates of the world—alpine, steppe, desert, subtropic rain forest, temperate, sea coast and many others. A second great factor of course has been history itself. The few gardens which have come down to us more or less intact from Colonial days emphasize two things: that though the European found many important plant materials when he landed in the New World (dahlias, zinnias, marigolds, kalmia, to mention but a few) he did not find any indigenous *garden forms*. These he brought with him. Whether he was English in New England, Dutch at New Amsterdam, German in Pennsylvania, French around New Orleans or Spanish at Santa Fe, the garden theme with which he was familiar had one basic pattern—the walled, geometrically designed plot of the Renaissance.

This basic Renaissance pattern is the skeleton on which all American gardens of the seventeenth and eighteenth centuries are constructed. The dooryard gardens of Boston no less than the patio of San Juan Capistrano in Southern California, the patios of New Orleans quite as much as the box parterres of Williamsburg, all show this common parentage. Naturally, there are variations. The Spanish, for example,

Continued on page 12

8

A modern reconstruction of a typical old New England dooryard garden,
this one in Stockbridge employs the forms and plant materials known
to have been popular in the eighteenth century. The house itself, built in
the 1740's by John Sergeant, was moved to its present location in 1928
and the garden was installed subsequently. Small and unpretentious
in both design and planting, it has a characteristic combination of
flowering stand-bys—iris, phlox, peony—and utilitarian herbs. With
its brick-paved, box-edged paths, this is the type of late Renaissance
garden cultivated throughout the English Colonies in the 1700's.

Stratford Hall, in Westmoreland County, is the ancestral home of the Lee family. One of the earliest of the great Virginia plantation houses, its gardens (left) have a sort of somber majesty quite in keeping with the house itself. Both the kitchen and the smoke house (at right in picture below) were entirely separate from main house.

Two Eighteenth Century Virginia Gardens

Stratford Hall: Home of the Lee Family
WESTMORELAND COUNTY, VIRGINIA

Gunston Hall: Home of George Mason
FAIRFAX COUNTY, VIRGINIA

PHOTOS BY DEMENTI

Gunston Hall, in Virginia, was the home of George Mason. Though the house itself is modest, the formal gardens, including the lowest terrace (shown above), are very extensive. The boxwood parterres, recently restored, are full of massed bloom all summer long.

"IT WAS with great difficulty," wrote Thomas Lee Shippen in 1790, on his first visit to his grandfather's house, Stratford, "that my uncles could persuade me to leave the hall to look at the gardens, vinyards, orangeries and lawns which surround the house." His reaction is not surprising, for there were few places like this outside England. Meticulously restored today by the Robert E. Lee Foundation, Stratford's house and gardens have a kind of somber splendor quite unlike other Virginia plantations either before or after it. The terraced gardens stem straight from the Late Renaissance parterre, with its rectangular patterns and terraced slopes. Based on the most careful archaeological excavations, these rebuilt gardens show a characteristic seventeenth century lack of interest in plant materials. Clipped boxwood, grass, and paved paths are the basic materials, just as they are at Versailles. Fruits, flowers, and vegetables were grown elsewhere on such an estate and were not considered activities worthy of public

view. Built in 1730, this is a garden for display like a tapestry on a wall or a fine carpet on a floor.

Built thirty years after Stratford, in 1759, Gunston Hall is architecturally smaller and less pretentious; but the formal garden, as reconstructed by the Garden Club of Virginia in 1953, is fully as extensive as that of Stratford and based on the same geometric designs. The house faces south, commanding a superb view of the Potomac River. The garden is organized in three terraces, the lowest one (above) overlooking the river directly. Thus, like Stratford, the garden is designed primarily to be seen from the house—a rich pattern unrolled like a carpet to act as a foreground to the natural view beyond. At Gunston Hall, however, the beds are filled with flowers known to have been popular during Mason's lifetime (1725–1792). And these give both color and variety to a design which is otherwise quite rigid. The entrance front on the north side was approached from the road along an avenue of clipped cherry trees.

11

Continued from page 8

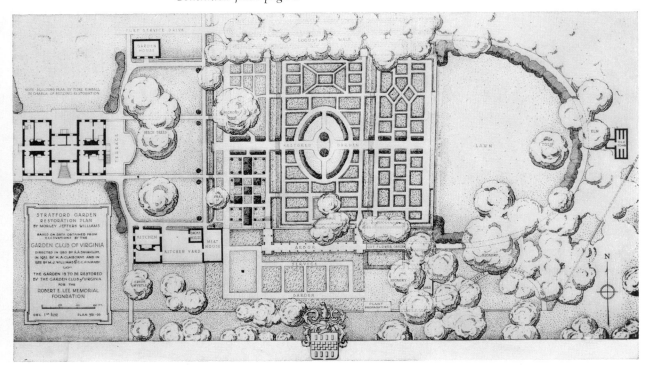

The difference between the Renaissance-inspired formal gardens of the eighteenth century and the romantic informality of the nineteenth is dramatized in these two plans. Stratford Hall (left) is laid out in patterns of precise geometry. But the 1840 design by A. J. Davis (right) goes to great pains to disguise its man-made origins, striving to simulate the accidental appearance and atmosphere of a natural landscape.

had learned from the Moors to place the garden in the center of the house—quite as excellent a climatic device for the land they came to as for the land they had left behind. The Bostonians used lilacs where the New Orleans French used oleanders. And hollyhocks appear in Philadelphia whereas yucca or mimosa were employed in the Southwest. But these are all minor variations on a single basic design theme.

Time, too, has dimmed the sharp outlines of many of these old gardens. For one that is maintained with truly archaeological precision, such as Mount Vernon, where all the plant material is kept at its original scale, there are dozens of so-called "shade gardens" around Natchez or Charleston which originally were just as sunny and tidily clipped as George Washington's. As a matter of fact few old gardens, even in Europe, are maintained at their original scale. Versailles is one exception to this creeping neglect—the French have kept the pleached *allées* at the same scale which the architect Lenôtre specified in the 1660's. But many other beautiful gardens of the same epoch owe their present charm to the fact that they were *not* kept in scale. One has only to compare Villa d'Este in Italy as it is today with seventeenth-century drawings of it to realize how much more effective it is with its present sixty-foot junipers than it was when those same cypress were clipped to a four- or five-foot hedge. Only the Japanese have consistently followed the tradition of planting a garden at full scale and then keeping it that way. For them this is essential since, for all its apparent artlessness, the

composition of a Japanese landscape is so carefully controlled that a single year's growth may destroy it.

The central characteristic of the Renaissance garden is, superficially, its formality. But this formality, in turn, is merely the expression of a very specific set of ideals for the landscape. It must be neat, balanced, orderly—in short, gardened. Its planes, patterns and shapes are those of geometry, not of nature; its forms are those of architecture, not of biology. In the topiary work of the High Renaissance, shrubs and trees are clipped into every conceivable shape—temples, clocks, swans, arcades—anything except their natural forms. It is not hard to see why, at the time of the Renaissance, men aspired to this kind of landscape. For them it marked the visible triumph of man over the raw and hostile forces of the natural world. And it is easy to understand why this type of garden became the very symbol of civilization to the men of the New World. For they encountered here the dark terrors of the forests, real and imagined: witches, werewolves, bears, Indians; swamps full of snakes and insects; endless prairies, stormy oceans, raging rivers. No wonder, then, that the walled or fenced and neatly patterned formal garden became the symbol of security, of civilized life itself.

This preference for Renaissance formality in garden and grounds was dominant throughout the first two centuries of American life. Late eighteenth-century estates such as Monticello or Mount Vernon com-

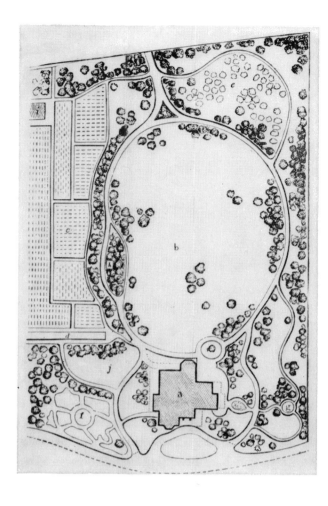

1730 when "Mrs. Lamboll excited great interest in the science of horticulture and gardening by planting a large and handsome flower and kitchen garden upon the European plan." The formal flower garden does not appear in the tidewater area until the eighteenth century. Of course, people grew flowers before then. Captain William Byrd was growing anemones, crocus and iris in 1684; but his son's famous house, Westover, was not built and landscaped until the 1740's. Also of the eighteenth century, or later, are the gardens of New Orleans and the Southwest.

Moreover, the formal pleasure garden, when it did appear, was often startlingly remote from the main house. Sometimes it was visible from the main living rooms, but more often not. Indeed, part of the pleasure of such a garden, apparently, was that it had to be walked to, and revealed itself only when one stepped through its enclosing hedge or wall. In plan it usually had some axial relationship to the main house. Sometimes this was clearly apparent, as in Andrew Jackson's home, The Hermitage, in Tennessee; but more often the connection was obscure.

Nature, as such, was not considered beautiful by the early Americans. Their letters and accounts abound in references to the richness of the soil, the wealth of the plant life, the fine building stones and precious metals. But there is scant reference to nature's beauty. As a matter of fact, this seems to have been a thoroughly European attitude toward the landscape: until it was neatly tilled and cultivated the land was not considered beautiful. On the contrary, as long as the forests were primeval, they were considered the haunts of all sorts of malign creatures—animals, barbarians and supernatural monsters. (The Italian word for foreigners is, even today, synonymous with forest dwellers. The Germans feared the forests. The English peopled them with all sorts of monsters.) And of course, for the early settlers, the forests were the source of greatest dangers—Indians and wild beasts.

The concept that the natural world, untouched by human hands, is a thing of beauty is very recent in Western history. Jean Jacques Rousseau with his "natural man" was one of the forerunners of the concept of nature as being the source of goodness and beauty. These new attitudes found their first expression in landscape design in England in the latter half of the eighteenth century when a number of remarkable gardeners, among them Batty Langley and Capability Brown, began to abandon the formal geo-

Continued on page 16

prised a whole complex of lawns, bowling greens, cutting and vegetable gardens, outhouses—including the ubiquitous "necessary house"—and the like. These are all at so large a scale that from some vantage points they may seem naturalistic in their relationship to each other. But the fact is that they, too, are rigidly Renaissance in their organization, stemming directly from the gardens that Andrea Palladio built in the sixteenth century for the Venetian aristocracy in the Po River Valley.

It would, however, be a great error to suppose that the formal pleasure garden in America appeared in full flower in the early days. It did not. It was a century or more in materializing: this for the good and sufficient reason that a pleasure garden is, socially, a great luxury and one of the last luxuries to be enjoyed in a new land. The first gardens were strictly utilitarian. William Wood, writing in 1634, describes the gardens of the new town of Plymouth: they are planted with "sweet sorrel, perrennial yarrow, hempe and flaxe, besides turnips, parsnips, carrots, radishes, musk mellions, cucumbers, onyons." In Boston, guests of Governor Winthrop could have "a private walk in his garden" as early as 1646, but we are not told what grew in it. Charleston's first flower garden dates from

The Gardens of Old Williamsburg

WILLIAMSBURG, VIRGINIA

F. S. LINCOLN

Although they are probably more exquisitely maintained today than they ever were in Colonial times, the private gardens of the Williamsburg Restoration give a vivid picture of the level of domestic amenity of the little capital in its heyday. They show a characteristic emphasis on overall design, a relative lack of interest in plants themselves.

As the capital of England's richest and most aristocratic colony in the New World, Williamsburg most accurately reflected in its architecture and gardens the tastes of Georgian England. As restored and reconstructed by a Rockefeller-endowed foundation, Williamsburg is therefore our largest and most persuasive museum of upper-class styles and tastes. Its reconstruction posed several fascinating problems in archaeology for, although decrepit, the old town was still alive when the work of restoration started in the early 1930's. Many historic houses and gardens had been either completely destroyed or altered beyond recognition in two centuries of continuous use. To restore them to their original condition meant exhaustive research.

F. S. LINCOLN

14

As is common in this sort of work, when documentation of actual conditions of a given building is not available, data from comparable buildings was used. Thus, a lost chandelier of which no records exist may be replaced by one known to have been used next door or popular during that time. Missing gardens are reconstructed on the basis of books known to have been in the possession of the owner. And lack of planting lists for the garden in question is circumvented by using those of known friends or neighbors.

In the hands of modern historians and archaeologists, such techniques make possible the reconstruction of a complete town like Williamsburg. But the chances are that the whole town has been subtly scaled up, in elegance and polish, beyond what it ever achieved at any time in its history. Certainly its productive aspects have entirely disappeared—the dye vats and pigpens, slave market and tanneries, cowlots and brick-kilns.

Yet, as a showcase of eighteenth-century concepts of domestic amenity and comfort, the Williamsburg Restoration is a valuable document. In its many scrupulously rebuilt and maintained gardens we have a glowing picture of baroque landscape design. The basic pattern is everywhere the same: the formal, intricately developed *parterre*, outlined in *Buxus suffruticosa*; the use of topiary work for vertical accents; the paved or graveled paths; and the relative lack of interest in plants themselves.

As might be expected, the gardens of the Governor's Palace are more extensive and more pretentious than the others. Indeed, with its handsome brick walls, monumental iron gates and barbered parterre, this garden must have seemed quite palatial to the colonists.

These are mostly pleasure gardens, designed primarily to be seen—often to be seen from afar. Hence their patterns are sharp, embroidered— much the same, in fact, as the patterns used in curtain and upholstery fabrics, even in clothing itself. To young Thomas Jefferson, weary of Georgian pomp and inefficiency, this baroque design was a "barbarous burthen" on society. And when the chance came his way, he discarded this type of designing altogether, substituting the majestic serenity of the Roman Revival. The difference between his University of Virginia campus and the Governor's Palace at Williamsburg is a measure of the difference between two periods.

15

Continued from page 13

metry of the Renaissance garden for the flowing, casual lines of nature. The distinguishing mark of this new school of naturalistic or informal garden design was the attempt to conceal man's handiwork.

The result was an idealized version of nature. The rolling lawns of England only appear to be natural. Actually an unmown meadow maintains this appearance merely for two or three weeks in early spring. If left alone for a season it springs up waist-high in meadow growth. And if unattended for several years in succession, it reverts quite rapidly to brush and then woodland. And the clumps of specimen plants which the designer of naturalistic gardens places here and there so artlessly, yet so artfully, are also idealizations of nature. Few of them are indigenous and all of them need continual care in the way of feeding and pruning to maintain maximum development. It is in this sense that the gardens of Langley and Brown may properly be called "romantic."

For the Western world, the English were the inventors of this type of garden design. In fact, the French—who were the first to borrow it—called it the "English" garden. But the concept is basically Oriental, and the appearance in England of the so-called Chinese and Japanese gardens during this same period establishes the genealogy. From the East, the Western gardener got two very important concepts, closely related to one another. The first was that nature itself was beautiful and good. Oswald Siren, the great specialist in Chinese art, has pointed out that in Chinese myth and legend nature has always been considered benign, the wilderness peopled not by enemies but by friends of man. For peace and security, one went to the forest primeval, not to the cloister or the walled town. Chinese painting reflects very accurately this attitude toward nature. The untouched landscape is its noblest subject matter.

The second concept was that if nature's landscapes are the most beautiful, the forms are to be literally imitated. Hence the level terrace, the vertical wall, the geometric patterns of boxwood and paving—all these obviously man-made forms—are abandoned in favor of naturalistic ones. Walls become rock gardens; formal fountains are converted into rock-edged brooks; level paving gives way to rolling lawns.

The romantic view of nature and its landscape expression, the informal garden, was not to become popular in the United States until after 1800. It reached its highest point of popularity in the 1830's and 40's. But there are already portents of it in the banjo-shaped bowling green at Mount Vernon (1785) or the western lawn of Monticello (ca. 1805). When Sir Basil Hall saw the Natchez gardens in 1827 he wrote home that "some . . . are laid out in the English, others in the French style."

One result of the growing popularity of the English garden was a wholly new sort of interest in horticulture. Plant material, after all, was of little significance in the Renaissance parterre. For all their visual splendor, the gardens of Versailles or the Luxembourg are planted with a very limited and ordinary collection of plants. The French—like the Spanish and Italians before them—would ruthlessly clip and pleach geraniums and trees into precise geometric forms. It was the total effect of plants and not their individual beauty or rarity which interested the Renaissance garden designer. The English garden, like the Oriental, accorded a much greater value to the character and beauty of individual plants. And an innovation of the period—the herbaceous border—displayed English ingenuity at its highest level. Here a wide variety of flowering plants were arranged for mass display, while at the same time their individual qualities were not only preserved but dramatized.

These two idioms of garden design, the formal and the informal, French and English, have formed the two extremes of American garden design ever since.

Among the strongest of the early horticultural influences toward naturalistic gardening in the New World was that of the Pennsylvania botanists. Where other plant hunters of the period collected solely for the purpose of shipping their finds to British and European botanists for identification and propagation, these Pennsylvanians established arboretums and gardens of native plants in and around Philadelphia. William Penn's interest in general gardening and especially in fruit and other trees was doubtless the initial cause for this early development of horticulture in his colony. He brought to it such men as his secretary James Logan (1674–1751), a fine gardener who is said to have given a start to John Bartram (1699–1776), a native of the New World, with little formal education, who became the outstanding Pennsylvania botanist. John Bartram's place on the Schuylkill River in Philadelphia is still preserved and attests by its rare surviving specimens to its builder's genius for horticulture. His many collecting expeditions along the eastern seaboard yielded plants which were shipped to England, but were also invariably planted in an informal manner in his own garden. His son William Bartram (1739–1823), author of the in-

Since the Spanish colonized only warm or semitropical areas in the New World, their most characteristic landscape device—the patio—was always suitable. They employed it in St. Augustine, Florida, as early as the 1590's. This patio, in the so-called Oldest House in the United States, is supposed to date from 1599. As restored today it shows the obvious additions of later periods but nevertheless represents the classic patio design—a central garden surrounded by a cool and shaded cloister.

valuable *Trails Through North and South Carolina, Georgia and E. and W. Florida,* followed in his father's footsteps. It was on one of his expeditions to the South that he collected the only known wild specimen of the lovely Franklinia tree, which was planted and propagated at Bartram's Gardens and thus saved for posterity.

Other Pennsylvania horticulturists who influenced the trend from formal to informal gardening included George Pierce, who became the first owner (in 1701) of the present Longwood Gardens near Wilmington, Delaware (he and his descendants planted many of the rare trees still standing today on this magnificent estate); John Evans (1790–1862) of Radnor, who in his plantings of Himalayan rarities imitated their

natural habitats; and Minshall (1801–1873) and Jacob Painter (1814–1876), who established the arboretum near Media which, after long neglect, has now been reclaimed as the John J. Tyler Arboretum. Here many fine specimens of Oriental spruce and yews and one fine *Sequoia gigantea* still attest to the skill and enthusiasm of the Painters.

This growing interest in plants as plants rather than merely as forms or as pigments with which to paint a landscape picture—either formal or informal —had a tremendous effect upon the development of gardening in America. New species and subspecies discovered by plant hunters in the New World were eagerly welcomed by the plantsmen of England and the Continent, who immediately set to work to develop from them horticultural selections and crosses. Such Americans shrubs as rhododendrons and azaleas, perennials like our native asters and phloxes, and many annuals, were so changed and improved that when, later on, they were sent back to the States by leading English and European firms, they were not commonly recognized by garden owners as being of American origin.

American nurserymen and seedsmen, during the

dens in the several areas where they sprang up. The three leading ones, quite naturally, were in the East— at Philadelphia, Boston and New York—and were organized respectively in 1827, 1829 and 1902. Many of the leading spirits in these organizations were expert plantsmen. Others were drawn to them because of the social prestige involved; but even these members, in most instances, had in their employ excellent gardeners—mostly from England and Scotland—

The Mission of San José, near San Antonio, Texas, followed the characteristic Spanish plan of building around enclosed cloisters or patios. Though the Mission itself dates from the seventeenth century, it was reconstructed in 1934–36. In the gardens proper, every effort has been made to re-capture the spirit of the old cloisters, which are used now, as they were then, for retreat and meditation by the priests. While the garden includes many traditional plants, no attempt has been made to confine it to Colonial botany. A deep red bougainvillea, in almost constant bloom, is a dominant source of color. Shrubs include hibiscus, queen's crown and the indigenous mountain laurel. A big live oak gives year-round shade.

early days, were more concerned with the development of new fruits and vegetables than they were with ornamental plants. Some of the early catalogs listed a greater number of varieties of apples and pears than are to be found today.

Three new influences in America, however, were to change all this emphasis on edibles. The first was the formation of horticultural societies in various parts of the country; the second, the advent of the garden club movement; and the third, the formation of the special flower societies—each devoted to the promulgation of its own favorite species.

The horticultural societies were originally founded and supported by the owners of estates and large gar-

often with dozens of trained assistants.

The era of the great estates had one by-product which turned out to be a considerable factor in stimulating widespread interest in gardening: the elaborate displays which the owners staged at the big spring flower shows held in many cities throughout the land. Rivalry for the various trophies and medals to be won at these affairs was intense, and no expense was spared in efforts to capture them. The owners of places of moderate size, of course, could not hope to compete, but they did enjoy the privilege of gleaning ideas which they could put to use and of gaining a much wider acquaintance with plant materials. The decline of this golden era of great estate displays at our big flower shows has unquestionably been a loss to American horticulture, but exhibits by national and state garden clubs, and by botanic gardens, have gradually been taking their place—in educational value, if not in interest to the non-gardening public.

The horticultural societies themselves, however, have suffered little from the passing of the big estates. Membership in these organizations has continued to grow; and although their activities have changed to

affiliated with any of the larger organized groups.

The third factor that has contributed, especially in the past few decades, to the present-day status of American gardening is what may be termed "special flower societies"—those whose devotees worship at a single shrine. One of the oldest of these is the American Rose Society, with 15,000 members. Remarkably, its nearest rival is the very young African Violet Society. Others pay homage to the chrysanthemum, the

In southern Texas, the Spanish conquistadores found much the same sort of climate—sunny and dry—which they left in Spain. Hence their patios were as necessary here as there for ameliorating the extremes of a semiarid region. The reconstructed Governor's Palace in San Antonio is a glowing representation of the charm of such areas. Here plants, water and paving combine to produce an area in which outdoor living is really feasible around the year. Controlled conditions make possible semi-tropical plants; papayas and bananas, pomegranates and figs, grapes and palms all flourish here. The result is a place of cool lushness, of relief from the sun, winds and dusts of the Texas landscape.

some extent, such changes have been in the direction of ever-widening and more democratic activities.

Of still greater impact upon the development of American gardens has been the growth of the garden club movement. The outstanding feature of this, as compared to similar movements in any other country, has been the fact that women, instead of men, have played the leading roles. Between them, the National Council of State Garden Clubs Inc., with a total membership of 350,000, and the Garden Club of America, with approximately 10,000 members, quite overshadow the Men's Garden Clubs of America with its 45,000 members. In addition to these three organizations, there are thousands of local clubs that are not

iris, the hemerocallis, the dahlia, the gladiolus, and a score of other species. Each is contributing its share to the betterment of American gardens.

All of these three great influences upon gardening in America—the horticultural societies, the garden clubs and the special flower societies—have tended to stimulate interest in plants themselves, as compared to the interest in garden design that was paramount in the older European gardens. But another, and perhaps even greater, force was at work to steer the evolving American garden into a course of its own—a course that has made the typical American garden of today out-looking instead of in-locking.

Throughout its history, the American pleasure garden has been conditioned by the special characteristics of American life. As in the evolution of all gardens everywhere, social and economic forces have played an important role in its evolving design. The pleasure garden is, by definition, a product of economic abundance. Only a relatively high standard of material well-being affords the possibility of devoting land, labor and money to an activity which, in narrow economic terms, is so "unproductive."

Economic well-being is no American monopoly. Since the fifteenth century, first Italy, then France and Spain, and lastly England have enjoyed periods of great wealth and prosperity. And it was precisely these

which is not only relatively prosperous but in which wealth is comparatively well distributed. The accidents of history have permitted us Americans, almost alone among the peoples of the earth, the luxury of this type of landscape. Even in Western Europe today, fenceless grounds and wall-less gardens are rare; in the Latin countries, unheard of. An Italian villa or French manor may sit in the center of grounds so large or so cleverly landscaped as to appear boundless. But the entire complex will be walled for psychic as well as actual security against marauders. Thus the French or Italian streetscape is as different from ours as possible: the street winds its way between walls so

Growing interest in horticulture in early America is attested by the erection, before 1809, of this privately-owned conservatory. Built on Manhattan by a Dr. Hosack, its heated glasshouses were full of many exotic plants so strange to Americans that they flocked to see them. It was many years before the cities themselves began to build municipally-owned botanic gardens.

periods which in each country produced the greatest gardens. And all of these gardens, with the partial exception of the English, have been enclosed, walled about, inward-turning: shut against the world at large. While borrowing from all of them, our own gardens have been distinguished by their openness, their facing outward toward neighbor and passerby. This tendency reaches its apogee in the typical prosperous suburb in America today, where the grounds of one house flow into those of its neighbors. Here the whole garden is on display. A wall or a fence would be considered an unneighborly act—and in many a suburb is actually forbidden by law.

Whatever the merit or lack of merit of such a suburban landscape, the fact remains that it is almost unique in the modern world. The only landscape which approaches it would be found in England; and even there, confining walls, fences and hedges are far more common. This American form is an expression of a socially peaceful countryside, of an economy

blind and high as to be forbidding. Only an occasional grilled gate gives a glimpse of the private pleasures beyond.

The manicured front lawn is almost exclusively an Anglo-American institution. In the American suburb this lawn is used as a setting to display the house, like velvet in a jewel casket. In most other parts of the world this practice would be found intolerable—a sacrifice of privacy quite as much as an invitation to thievery. With the growing mechanization of American life and the absolute domination of our streets and roads by noisy and dangerous automobiles, there is a growing feeling among Americans that this "showcase" type of landscape design is losing whatever validity it might have had.

But the American "open garden" is merely the complement of the American "open house." Except for New Orleans and the Southwest, where Latin influence introduced the inward-turning house around a central patio, our typical house plan has always been one in which all rooms face outwards toward the street and the neighbors. Psychologically, this type of plan has a twofold significance. On the one hand it indicates an active interest in the outside world—the desire to "see what's going on"; and an equally positive, if less admirable, desire to be seen and admired by the neighbors. But there was functional justification for the large doors and window openings which usually accompanied the front lawn. In the northern climates of our country they admit winter sun; in the South they permit summer ventilation. Of course, large glass areas in the North also are wasteful of heat; hence, the storm sash and weather-strip were invented. And in the South the unshaded window admits sun as well as breeze; hence the continuous porch or gallery was developed as a shading device.

Fancy and fact have thus coincided to make American windows steadily larger, until today an entire wall—even an entire building—of glass is a commonplace. Such transparency obviously gives a wholly new importance to the garden and the landscape in general. They become, in effect, an integral part of the room itself, with its uncluttered simplicity and atmosphere of serenity. This, more than anything else, explains the great interest in Japanese gardens today, since the Japanese with their sliding walls have for centuries done away with the ironclad division between indoors and out.

But the glass wall ("picture window," in popular terminology) exposes the strange ambivalence of today's American house-owner; does he want to see or be seen? There is no such paradox in Japanese house-and-garden design. The garden is for the exclusive enjoyment of the family and its visitors. It can be seen only from the house and is completely screened from the outside world. On the other hand, the average American house, especially the "real estate development" or the "project" house, often has picture window walls which open directly onto the street, the neighbor's garage or even onto the neighbor's picture window. There is seldom a "picture" to be seen from today's picture window—at least from the inside out. But, from the outside in, these windows are increasingly draped and accoutered in a fashion that reveals the less admirable mores of domestic architecture. More and more they seem like department store windows intended for display.

Perhaps the most important point of all is that throughout our history there has been a steady democratization of the pleasure garden. In Washington's day it was more or less the prerogative of the wealthy country gentleman or of the city merchant prince. Only such gentry were able to afford the labor, the imported seeds and bulbs, the European garden books which were essential to professionally competent landscape gardening. Undoubtedly, lesser folk had dooryard gardens modeled on this pattern but they would have maintained a semi-utilitarian character, vegetables and herbs, rather than flowers and ornamental shrubs, being dominant. With the nineteenth century and the rise of the urban middle classes, all this began to change. More and more people could afford flower gardens as sheer recreational or (as we should call it today) leisure-time activities. The rise of the horticultural press and the appearance of large-scale commercial seedsmen and nurserymen is a measure of this process. By the early twentieth century the number of garden amateurs was legion and the garden club era well under way: the democratization of the pleasure garden was complete.

The very wealthy meanwhile continued the development of the great landscaped estate, modeled more and more on the English prototype. The estate, by its scale and complexity, demanded not only professional landscape architects to design it but professional gardeners to maintain it. The estate movement reached its peak in the years between 1890 and the Great Depression of the 1930's. Since that time it has seen a steady decline. One by one, the great establishments all across the country—at Palm Beach, Newport, Long Island, Grosse Pointe and Santa Barbara—have been disappearing. The reasons for this are many and complex. Obviously, the rising cost and increasing scarcity of skilled garden labor is one; another is the great expansion of our cities, with their increasing pressure on suburban land. But whatever the causes, the results are the same: irrespective of its price, the American house stands on a steadily shrinking plot.

With this decrease in size comes a parallel increase in the intensity of use and development of the plot. As a matter of fact, our attitude toward the *use* of a garden has undergone a qualitative change in the past decade. Traditionally, the pleasure garden was designed to be seen, either from the house (Japan) or from the street (United States). It was not thought of as being useful space which could be lived in. Today's concept of "outdoor living" thus involves a new set of functional criteria for garden design. And thus we find the modern garden being planned and built like the modern house. Attention is focused on comfort (summer shade, winter sun), privacy, easy circulation, easy maintenance. Old forms disappear.

Continued on page 24

21

The Gardens
of
Mt. Vernon

Home of George Washington
MT. VERNON, VIRGINIA

*The vegetable garden at Mt. Vernon today is
as close to the state in which Washington left
it as a century of research and care can make it.*

I⟨T WAS⟩ not an Act of Congress that preserved for us the home of George Washington. It was rather an act of foresight on the part of a Victorian spinster, Anne Pamela Cunningham. She conceived the idea of forming an organization of women to preserve Mt. Vernon—then falling into ruin under the ownership of the General's great-grandnephew, John Augustine Washington. Ever since 1859 it has been under the management of the Mt. Vernon Ladies Association.

As it stands today, Mt. Vernon represents one of our earliest, as well as one of our best, examples of

domestic archaeology. The preservation is doubly valuable: first for its priceless historical significance; secondly, for the light it throws on late eighteenth-century architectural and horticultural practices.

Fortunately for posterity, the development of the house and grounds at Mt. Vernon is extremely well documented. Washington was not only a passionate gardener but also a careful record-keeper. Thus there is scarcely a tree or a shrub whose exact variety and location he did not record, and hardly any aspect of farm or garden maintenance that he did not investigate. We know from the records of his library that he kept abreast of all the literature from England on landscaping and horticulture.

Mt. Vernon came to George Washington by inheritance in 1752, and he made it his home until his death in 1799. Both the house and the grounds received continual improvement and refinement under his ownership. And it is clear from the documents that the developments were all made according to an overall plan which Washington had worked out at a fairly early date. This plan is essentially Palladian—a great house flanked on either side by lower service wings which curve forward to form an entrance court for the long ap-

*As the oldest restoration in
America, Mt. Vernon's plantings
have reached magnificent maturity.*

PHOTOS BY SAMUEL CHAMBERLAIN

proach from the highway. There is nothing casual or informal about this scheme. Basically, it is a Late Renaissance design in which one element balances the other with the precision of a minuet.

Yet for all its formality, the layout of Mt. Vernon was highly functional for its times. Its master was actually head of a small manufacturing village. Dairy, kitchens, tailor and shoe shops, carpentry, spinning and weaving—all that the family ate and much that it wore and used were processed within earshot of Washington's study. Any plan that could accommodate this wide range of operations and still preserve an appearance of order and grace was obviously an effective plan.

As an internationally famous figure and inveterate correspondent on all matters horticultural, Washington obviously had access to a much wider range of plant materials from all over the world than most of his contemporaries. As early as 1759 he was ordering glass bells from London for early forcing. He was sprouting mahogany seeds in trays in 1785, as well as trying to acclimatize West Indian acacias and Florida palmetto to Virginia. He had one of the first glasshouses in the country, and was a great hand at grafting and training fruit trees *espalier*. For such reasons, the gardens at Mt. Vernon (vegetable and flower alike) display a far wider range of material than is common to other great gardens of that epoch.

George Washington was, of course, a man of great wealth: the Mt. Vernon home farm contained 8,000 acres at his death. But wealth alone never produced a fine garden. Knowledge, taste and devotion are also required; and Washington lavished all of these on his homeplace until the very year of his death.

The walled flower gardens at Mt. Vernon balance those for vegetables.
A horticulturist with a world-wide correspondence, Washington was able to
grow a far wider range of flowers, fruits and vegetables than his neighbors.

Continued from page 21

The baroque traceries of these box-edged flower beds at Mt. Vernon create much the same pattern as is found in the wallpapers, damask and velvets of the period.

SAMUEL CHAMBERLAIN

Front yard, side yard, and back yard are becoming obsolete. The ubiquitous "patio" takes over. In short, the whole plot tends to become a garden and the garden to become an integral part of the house.

In view of the changing social and economic conditions already described this is an eminently logical solution for the typical suburban house. Largely because of the automobile, the street has become as unattractive and hazardous as it was in medieval times. But since the house is tied to the auto, it cannot get away from it. Hence, in those instances where privacy is wanted, we see a tendency to return to the walled (or the screened) garden, with a house at or near the center—the same basic plan as that used by the Romans at Pompeii or the Chinese in old Peking. Even if the front lawn remains community property along the street or road, the more the garden-for-living is lived in, the greater becomes the need for privacy.

But before the grounds of the American house could be thus radically revised, a whole series of technological advances had to be made. The grounds of a middle-class home in the Civil War days were divided into front and back "yards" (just as the house itself was divided into front and back rooms) for the good and sufficient reason that many unbeautiful auxiliaries were essential to running the house. The "necessary house" (as the Virginians termed it), clothesline, washpots, woodpile, cowbarn, and chicken run; a stable and perhaps a pigsty and a smokehouse had to be provided. These were neither beautiful to look at, to smell nor to hear. They required a lot of space

but, for convenience, they had to be near the house. Of course, in the homes of the rich, with household slaves (such as the Washingtons or the Lees maintained, or with a staff of servants like that of the Vanderbilts), such service areas could be remote from the main house. But for the ordinary family, with little or no household help, the facilities could be neither remote nor beautified. Not until all these services could be industrialized or mechanized would it be possible to think of beautifying any more than the front, or public half, of the plot.

This mechanization had been substantially accomplished by the opening years of the twentieth century. Municipal water had banished the well and pump house. Plumbing and municipal sewage had banished the outhouse. The automobile had replaced the horse; gone were pasture and stable. A modern food industry had made obsolete cowbarn, pigpen and chicken run, along with the vegetable garden and orchard. Inside the house, electricity and gas had revolutionized all those household chores that did not lend themselves to being removed to the factory.

The importance of this technological revolution, its impact upon the American house and garden, cannot be overestimated. It has made practical, for the first time in history, the contemporary idea of placing the house, even a modest house, in the center of a garden. It has demolished old concepts of front and back, indoors and out, and resulted in the possibility of our establishing and enjoying an entirely new kind of domestic beauty.

Treasury of American Gardens

Masterpiece in Tulips and Azaleas

Sherwood Gardens: John W. Sherwood

BALTIMORE, MARYLAND

IF ADAPTION to site and climate are the marks of a good garden, then Sherwood Gardens clearly ranks high. It is designed primarily for spring bloom—the one reliable season in the southeastern United States, where extremely hot summers make first-rate summer bloom almost impossible. Lawns and herbaceous borders, those standbys of cooler areas such as New England and the Pacific Northwest, are thus expensive and hazardous—and this owner has wisely avoided building the gardens around them. He has shown a similar wisdom in the development of the site. When he began, twenty-five years ago, the setting was rolling woodland: red, black and white oak and some swamp cypress from fifty to seventy-five years old. This character has been carefully preserved.

The gardens as they stand today consist essentially of a network of grass paths between the trees, edged with pansies, tulips (about 100,000 of all varieties), and azaleas (about 10,000). Behind these borders are planted flowering crabs and pink and white dogwood. Behind the planting stands the forest itself. Such a scheme produces enchanting color in April and May, and an extremely handsome landscape around the year.

Sherwood Gardens is all the more remarkable in that it has been completely designed by the owner, with no professional assistance. "We began," says Mr. Sherwood, "in a very modest fashion. Today, the gardens cover seven acres. They are bounded on four sides by roads, so that people may drive around and get a splendid view." However, the owner is hospitable and each spring thousands of visitors wander through the gardens at will.

"We have found that the soil lends itself splendidly to the production of azaleas and tulips," Mr. Sherwood says. "With the azaleas we have used tons and tons of leaf mold, rotted oak in particular. For the tulips we use a rather light soil, with some sand added and, at planting time, bone meal."

All of the thousands of azaleas were small plants when put in but they have grown to heights of eight to ten feet and diameters up to eight. They include Japanese, Korean, Chinese and Dutch varieties. Outstanding among them is *Japonica alba*, *Ledifolia rosea* and Damask Rose. There are also thousands of the *Kaempferi* in nearly all its shades.

The owner has other horticultural interests. He has collected old boxwood for years and he also has an evergreen rock garden. But the exceptional quality of Sherwood Gardens is the brilliant way in which it works with existing conditions of site, soil and climate.

Massed plantings of azaleas are woven through a lightly-shaded woodland of native trees. Tulips and pansies are grouped in the foreground. The evergreens are native cedar (Juniperus virginiana) clipped into columnar form.

*This typical vista shows Sherwood's basic pattern: a flowing grass path cut
through the indigenous woodland and banked on either side with azaleas
of many species and all colors. Massed pansies and tulips add interest.*

Rear Admiral and Mrs. Albert C. Read (le
WASHINGTON, D.C.

Mrs. Willcox Auchincloss (right)
WASHINGTON, D.C.

*The skillful way in which a narrow rectangle
has been transformed is apparent
in this view, seen from the parlor floor.
The flowing lines of the new raised terrace
in the foreground and the curving
brick paths broaden its apparent width
and at the same time reduce its length.*

THESE two reconstructed gardens give dramatic evidence of what can be accomplished even within the awkward confines of the long narrow lots common in the older residential sections of many eastern cities. Such gardens originally were almost always centered by a rectangular grass plot bordered by a flagstone path; narrow beds were then backed against high enclosing walls. Such a design merely aggravated the already unpleasing shape of the garden. In both cases here, the landscape architects have softened the shape by a deliberate asymmetric pattern of paving, grass and planting; by concentrating the paved areas near the house, to form useful terrace areas; and by dividing the garden laterally to minimize its apparent length.

In the case of the Read garden (above) the levels have remained unchanged—that is, the terrace opens off the parlor floor. But in the case of the Auchincloss garden the levels have been adroitly manipulated to lower the landscaping to the level of a formerly half-buried basement floor. By giving this room a glass wall and enlarging the former areaway to the dimensions of a comfortable

Style in Town Gardens

terrace, a wholly new and much more satisfactory relationship between house and garden has been established. The basement floor becomes a garden floor; and even when viewed from the upper level of the old parlor floor, the new levels of the garden provide a much handsomer view than formerly.

Plant material in both gardens is simple and hardy—such stand-bys of this region as dogwood, box, azaleas and ivy. Spring bloom such as tulips and pansies are followed by potted plants for summer color. But gardens like these are wisely based more upon structure than bloom. The result is year-round interest, won with a minimum of maintenance and repair.

A glass wall opening out onto the newly-excavated sunken terrace converts a half-buried basement into this delightful garden room. Planting is simple and sturdy; the effect comes mostly from architectural features such as the retaining walls of old brick, the boundary fences of unpeeled cedar stakes.

The Auchincloss garden, seen here from the old parlor floor, has been divided transversely into three sections. This serves to conceal its awkward shape, making it much more attractive visually. But the subdivision into three parts is functional as well: the lowest level (left foreground) is paved for outdoor entertaining; the center section is given over to lawn and flowers; the rear, partially screened by planting, is a graveled play yard for children. Such separation of function is as important in the garden as in the house.

29

PHOTOS BY RICHARD GARRISON

On the Ruins of an Old Powder Mill

"Eleutherean Mills": Mrs. Francis B. Crowninshield

MONTCHANIN, DELAWARE

OFTEN, a fine garden grows out of the ruins of some earlier project—an older garden, the remains of some old structure. This is especially true in Europe, where a garden of today often represents the accumulated accidents of a long history. This accidental quality in a landscape is hard to define and almost impossible to fabricate out of the whole cloth—though a century and more ago the synthetic, moss-covered ruin was tried repeatedly. But, real or false, such gardens are rare in America; this one, based on an old powder works of E. I. du Pont, must be unique.

The gardens here were begun in 1919 by Mrs. Crowninshield and her husband, without professional assistance. Their primary interest was to preserve whatever remained of the original masonry structures. These dated from the early 1800's and had been, through the years, covered with various structures of corrugated iron. The first step was to remove these later accretions completely. The new garden was then laid out around whatever remained in the way of walls, foundations or basements.

That these remnants laid the basis for an astonishingly effective garden is obvious from the photographs. What is less apparent is the work which went into its construction. It took better than six years, not only because the owners did the planting themselves but because they wished, like archaeologists, to supervise all excavations of the ruins.

Some of the devices are little short of inspired. The pools, for instance, which today reflect the

Columnar cedars, classic sculpture, boxwood and paving—formal materials, all of them—are used in a most informal manner. Note the way the flagged terrace is interplanted with rock garden plants. This gives a riot of spring color and eliminates any problems of summer maintenance, when owners are away.

30

PHOTOS BY GOTTLIEB HAMPFLER: F.P.G.

The roofless colonnade and weathered classic sculptures give an air of elegiac splendor to these quiet pools and ivy-covered walls. Yet in both design and execution the garden is simple. The walls are those of a ruined factory, the pools merely its flooded basements.

classic fragments of sculpture and columns, were originally the basements of the old mill houses. The ground plan of the factory is thus preserved with complete accuracy while furnishing the basic pattern of a lovely garden complex.

Wisdom was shown in other matters as well. The owner spends only short periods in this house —some eight weeks in spring and four in the fall. Thus all bloom and color is scheduled for these two periods. Moreover, all plant material was selected with naturalization in mind, so that maintenance is held to a minimum. For the same reason, a great deal of paving was used in areas which normally would be put down in grass.

The result is definitely romantic. The garden vistas have a nostalgic air, an echo of the past, which is strengthened by the absence of clipped lawns and tailored beds.

31

Back-yard Garden

for

Spring and Fall

Mr. and Mrs. William Hurd Hill
WASHINGTON, D.C.

*The quiet, formal pattern of pool, paths and flower beds makes
this rebuilt garden pleasant to look at and easy to maintain.*

THE town houses of the eastern seaboard during the early 1800's were almost invariably built right on the street; their gardens were usually in the rear. This was a wise provision for peace and privacy in those days. Today, when automobile traffic has made urban streets noisy, dirty and dangerous, it is almost an essential in the city garden. Thus this reconstructed back garden in downtown Washington, D.C., is thoroughly up to date despite its age. Its layout is formal and familiar—

brick-paved paths, geometric beds and central pool, with the brick paving widened to provide a space for outdoor sitting in pleasant weather. Since the house is closed during the summer months, the garden is used only in spring and fall. The landscape architect, Miss Rose Greely, has concentrated on spring bloom and evergreen foliage. Thus in bad weather the garden presents a pleasing view to the rooms that overlook it and in good weather a valuable area for outdoor dining.

Radiance in a Sheltered Garden

"Elton": Mr. and Mrs. J. Dudley Clark

WILMINGTON, DELAWARE

ENTIRELY aside from its beauty, the walled garden is an important horticultural tool, suitable to widely different types of climates. It was used throughout the Arab and Spanish worlds as a means of creating shade, coolness and moisture in hot or desert regions. By excluding torrid sun, dry-ing winds and dust, it created a small, cool "micro-climate" in which plants—and people—could flourish.

But the walled garden has also been widely used in northern Europe and Great Britain for exactly opposite reasons—to trap the sunshine, exclude

To keep a garden as large as this in continuous bloom throughout the season requires both hard work and careful planning. Shown here in its late spring splendor of Darwin tulips, bearded iris and purple wisteria, this garden has a complex and carefully worked out sequence of bloom.

Concert of Gardens

"*Appleford*": Mrs. Lewis H. Parsons
VILLANOVA, PENNSYLVANIA

APPLEFORD is a spacious, eighteen-acre country place which boasts just about every landscape feature imaginable: meadows, woodland, duck ponds, waterfalls, brooks and a swimming pool. There is, in addition, a system of paved terraces and specialized gardens arranged around the house like rooms: a small boxwood garden (see next page); a rose garden; a walled garden connect-

After the burst of spring bloom—all of it from hardy plants, shrubs and trees—Appleford settles down as a predominantly shady green garden. Two exceptions are the rock-wall garden (right) which is planted with pink geraniums and white caladiums for summer color; and the garden above, where beds of white petunias follow others of white tulips.

ing house to swimming pool; and a garden of flowering shrubs. Finally, there are extensive wildflower gardens, rock-wall plantings and dogwood and lilac walks.

Yet this is not a professionally-run "estate." On the contrary, it is largely the result of the enthusiastic labors of the owner, who has for thirty-five years been at work developing the grounds. As it stands today, the house is a handsome example of old-style Pennsylvania masonry. It consisted originally of three farm buildings, dating from 1705 to 1795, which were remodeled into one by the architect Brognard Okie. When the Parsons bought it, there were no gardens at all, merely meadow and woodland. Everything else, including the white pines and the dogwood which line the approach from the highway, is the work of the owners.

Moreover, most of the construction was done by the gardener with unskilled local labor. And of all the plant material, very little came from commercial sources: most of it, says Mrs. Parsons, they propagated themselves. (The boxwood garden, for example, contains twelve old plants which they bought, and 5,000 which they rooted!) Even the old handmade bricks which are used in garden paths, terrace pavings and walls were collected in and around Independence Hall in Philadelphia.

As might be guessed, the successful completion of a project such as this is the result of horticultural good sense; and the maintenance of the grounds today shows the same sort of judgment. Though Appleford is a year-round residence, the gardens are designed for early bloom only—that is, from April to July. There is no summer bloom or cutting garden, which would require constant maintenance and replanting. The only exception to this is the boxwood garden, which is bedded first with white tulips and then with white petunias; and the long dry wall (see illustration) which, after the spring bloom of white, blue and yellow, is planted along the base with pink geraniums and caladiums.

The small gardens around the house are shaded and cool all summer long. From July on, their color comes from potted plants which Mrs. Parsons uses in profusion: standard heliotrope, fuchsias, geraniums and tuberous begonias.

The approach to the house is along a pleasant drive, marked by a series of changing vistas like these—such vistas as only time and care can produce. The gardens proper are concentrated around the house itself.

This courtyard garden is frankly derivative in design, with its central fountain and geometric pattern echoing European cloisters. Basic planting is boxwood, ivy and yew, with potted plants for summer color.

A Touch of the Elizabethan

B. D. Phillips

BUTLER, PENNSYLVANIA

With the rising acceptance of contemporary design, the tendency to duplicate or re-create the forms of old gardens from other lands has all but disappeared. So-called "period design" in landscaping, as in architecture, is a thing of the past. But twenty-five years ago, when this estate was laid out, modern architecture was still a thing of the future. Given the reference frame of Elizabethan England, the designers have here created an impressive complex.

Like all Renaissance and Renaissance-inspired designs, these are "pleasure gardens" in the truest sense of the term. And designed, above all, to give pleasure to the eye. They are also, as plan and pictures reveal, essentially architectural in their character. Walls, garden houses, terraces and pools are the dominant elements in the design. Plant material, while handsome—especially after years of care—is of secondary interest. Architectural elements are, of course, expensive and this is perhaps one of the major reasons for their disappearance from the American scene. But they date from a period in which expense was a secondary consideration. And they have created a kind of monumental splendor which, within its own terms, is admirable.

42

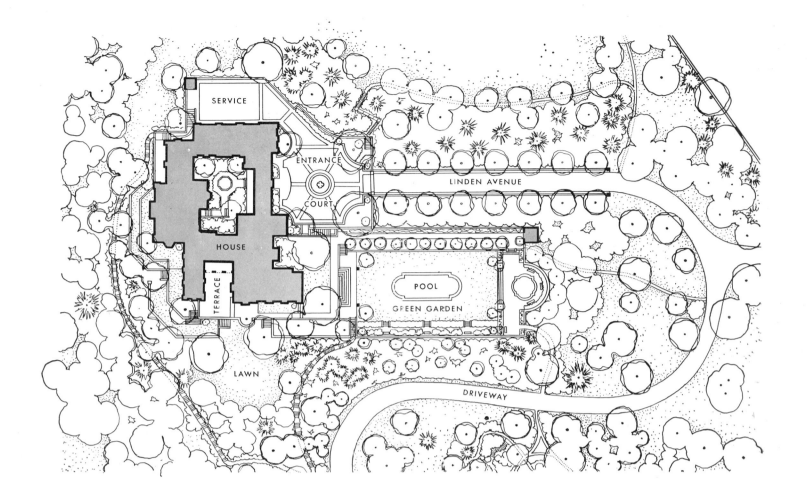

Like the great English gardens, this Pennsylvania place has been developed
in an architectural direction. The landscape has been sculptured into a
series of interlocking terraces which are an extension of the house
itself. Plant material has been selected almost like furniture for a room
—that is, for its permanent shape, structure and color. Here, perfect
maintenance and control of form are mandatory.

In contrast to its formal garden, the rest of the Whitney estate is developed in an informal fashion. The rolling woodlands have been handled in two ways: around the pond underbrush has been cleared and trees cut down to open vistas and permit dogwood to reach full size.

These conditions are met on a fairly large estate where professional gardeners assure top-quality maintenance and there is a variety of areas for outdoor activities of all sorts.

A large part of the rest of the grounds is landscaped in a casual, naturalistic manner (see above), thus offering a pleasing relief to the more formal sections. Here natural contours, native growth and existing trees have been preserved. Because of the dogwood and naturalized spring bulbs, these areas are most colorful in spring but they are pleasant to walk through around the year.

In wooded areas adjacent to the house, trees have been thinned out to allow for a regularly mowed lawn. This creates a transition zone between the formal areas and the woodland beyond. Such a treatment is relatively maintenance-free and produces handsome vistas around the year.

PHOTOS BY BEIDLER-VIKEN

Mellow and Varied

Mrs. Richard M. Tobin
SYOSSET, LONG ISLAND, N.Y.

This Long Island estate offers a delightful variety of gardens, each with its superb vistas and its foreground of rich color. A long, naturalistic pool with wooded banks reflects the treetops in its depths and is approached by a rustic, gently curving path of fieldstone interplanted with grass and bordered by a spring flood of various moisture- and shade-loving flowers. Clumps of Japanese Iris extend to the very edge of a pool, and the human visitor is tempted to follow them by a path which leads eyes and footsteps toward the water.

Another garden, open to the sun, is devoted principally to long, curving borders of tulips edged with box. In sharp contrast to the moist, woodsy quality of the pool planting, the tulip garden is accented by flowering fruit trees and dogwoods. A very unusual and practical feature is a curving, box-edged grass path between the tulip borders and the perennial garden, where doronicum, Oriental Poppies and peonies await their turn to carry on as the tulips fade. Vine-clad wattle fences make a pleasing background for the perennials, keep the eye from straying into other planted areas and at the same time stimulate the curiosity of the visitor to see what lies beyond.

This is clearly an old garden, one which has grown more mellow with the years—as its glorious azaleas (see bottom of next page), reaching heights approaching those of young trees, testify. The shrubbery, though perhaps too exuberant in some places, is witness to the care lavished on it through the seasons.

This luxuriant growth gives an air of naturalness which is sadly lacking in many plantings of flowering shrubs dominated by azaleas. Too often the glorious color masses, unrelieved by sufficient foliage, produce an effect of studied artificiality.

GOTTSCHO SCHLEISNER

For all its charming casualness, such a wild garden as this takes great skill in design and construction to be wholly successful. Once properly built and planted, however, it is long-lived and needs little care. As in most wild gardens, the bloom is primarily a springtime affair. Scillas, primulas, foam-flowers and dozens of others are massed in sheets of color along the water's edge. By midsummer this color is for the most part replaced by masses of ferns and foliage plants.

Topiary work—the art of training and clipping evergreen plants into the forms of birds and beasts—was a favorite of Renaissance garden designers. One of the few surviving examples of topiary in this country is to be found on the Oakleigh Thorne estate in Millbrook, New York.

Another of the main features is an *allée* of maples trimmed high in the French manner, and bordered by a series of enclosed beds edged with box—the general effect being reminiscent of the formal gardens around the Governor's palace at Williamsburg.

In the less formal parts of the gardens, naturalistic pools have been used with a pleasing simplicity that adds much to the general atmosphere of serenity. Surrounded by emerald-green turf and framed by azaleas, evergreens and large deciduous trees, the water lies like an uncut jewel.

Richness in a Little Space

Mr. and Mrs. Alexander Kouzmanoff

PORT CHESTER, NEW YORK

WHEN money, land and time are unlimited, a good garden is not too difficult to come by. But when all three of them are limited, as they were here, a garden as successful as this is truly an accomplishment. Designed and largely built by the owners in the last six years, on an average-sized suburban lot, it is an excellent example of the integration of house and garden. Indeed, they are so intimately tied together that it is difficult to determine where one leaves off and the other begins. At the same time, the design is so skillfully composed that the plot appears much more spacious than it is, and yet maintains privacy around its boundaries.

In planning his garden, the owner's chief concerns were two: to have the maximum of usable, outdoor living space for the seven months of use which the climate permits; and to have maximum beauty around the year, even in those months when the garden can only be enjoyed from indoors.

The site of the house, which was part of a real estate development, had several assets and a number of liabilities. The assets were: a glass-walled living room on the rear or garden side; a fairly steep slope up from the house in this direction; and a clump of handsome trees along the rear property line. The liabilities were: run-off from this slope during heavy rains; lack of privacy from neighbors; no developed terraces, porches or other areas for outdoor living. The assets were conserved and the liabilities overcome by converting the slope into a series of related terraces stepping up the hillside. These were connected by walks and rock gardens, the latter planted with shrubs—dogwood, laurel, black alder—and wildflowers, most of them moved in from the woods beyond. Around the house at the level of the main floor are several other terraces, all paved, one uncovered, one trellised and

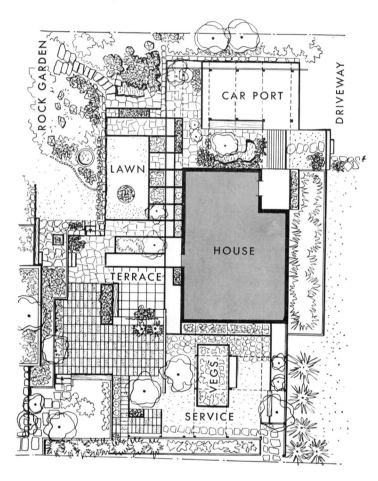

one roofed over with translucent plastic. Each of these is screened and planted so effectively that during warm weather, when they would be most used, they give the sense of privacy and enclosure that is usually achieved only on much more spacious grounds.

The owner feels that one of his most successful undertakings has been the use of paving materials —in some cases together with shadow-throwing lattice work—to join house and garden still more completely. Another accomplishment was getting a number of views of the garden, all different,

The lawn outside the glass-walled living room is here seen from the paved dining terrace with its grill for outdoor cooking. Beyond the living room is a loggia which in the wintertime is used as a carport.

The plot plan shows clearly how a small subdivision lot has been developed to give a wide variety of outdoor areas for all sorts of specialized use, including vegetable-growing and clothes-drying. They give the illusion of great space, and at the same time are screened from street and neighbors.

The loggia off the living room (below) is roofed with a wooden treillage which carries a translucent waterproof plastic roof. Ideal for summer evenings, this loggia is used in wintertime as a carport, since the "wall" toward the street is actually a garage door.

PHOTOS BY KONSTANTIN J. KOSTICH

View down the slope toward the living room side of the Kouzmanoff house. A series of low terraces, supported by dry-built rock walls, has been carved out of the natural slope. These walls are planted with a wide assortment of perennials and annuals for all-season color. Note the trellised carport-loggia to left of living room.

from the house and the living terrace. The service area and the small garden at the carport entrance are convenient, yet each is inconspicuously screened off from the garden living area by means of plants, wood fences and angles in the paths.

Intelligent planning and the clever use of screens, both living and inanimate, have succeeded in making this place look several times as large as it actually is, and in creating a variety of engaging vistas.

A louvered wood fence screens the service areas from the dining terrace. Here, as elsewhere, the plot has been subdivided into a series of outdoor rooms so as to give a choice of sun or shade, breeze or calm.

PHOTOS BY KONSTANTIN J. KOSTICH

Looking down the garden front of the house from the dining terrace. The pergola here gives the right amount of shading for a bright summer's day. For outdoor dining in cooler weather or for use at night there is a paved terrace with barbecue pit up the hill to the left.

Frame for a
Waterscape

Estate of Nelson Doubleday
MILL NECK, LONG ISLAND, N.Y.

THIS garden on a large Long Island estate is a particularly happy blending of the formal and informal, uniting a traditional residence with a surrounding natural landscape. As the family is often away during much of the summer, the accent has been placed on spring effects.

The site posed the problem of obtaining privacy and at the same time taking full advantage of the distant view, including a beautiful waterscape of Long Island Sound. This has been solved by grading and by the use of retaining walls to form a comparatively level space adjacent to the house; also by the use of walls and hedges about the garden in such a way as to secure a commanding view of the sound. The removal of tall trees insures an unobstructed view of the water. The substitution of low-growing species enhances the vista with a lovely frame.

The general design of the garden is simple and so planned as to require a minimum of upkeep. The planting beds are edged with dwarf box allowed to grow naturally; and the walks are of random paving, set flush, with grass chinks, permitting the use of a lawn mower. Turf areas are small and rectangular, thus allowing for easy maintenance.

Among the special features of this garden, one of the most interesting is the use of pergolas covered with hardy vines of various types to form frames for a succession of views within the garden itself and also for distant vistas. Although especially suited to this garden, this device is one that could well be used more generally. To support roof members, attractive permanent brickwork has been utilized here instead of the more common wood columns, which are often out of keeping with their surroundings and are always subject to sagging and eventual decay. Of the same material as the house walls, the brick columns here help to join house and garden harmoniously.

The enclosing hedges, while providing the required privacy, are kept clipped to desired dimensions, and so treated as to be unobstructive and to avoid a walled-in effect. The placement of small trees at intervals inside the confines of the garden unites it visually with the landscape beyond, thus further reducing any feeling of sharp separation between the two.

The plant material is notable for its simplicity. As we see the garden here—in mid-May, after the color of spring-flowering bulbs has gone—the outstanding features are pink and white dogwood, azaleas and rhododendron, with wisteria just coming into bloom atop the pergolas. The colors have been held to soft tones of pink and lavender combined with white to form a restful harmony in a low key.

A climbing hydrangea frames this picture of box-edged borders backed by a sheared hemlock hedge.

GOTTSCHO-SCHLEISNER

57

Grass, a few shrubs, trees, and some ground cover work a miracle in a city yard.

A City Retreat

Mrs. Natalie Bowen

NEW YORK CITY

Taking a small, shaded back-yard area of poor, hard soil located in the Greenwich Village section of Manhattan, the owner, in a relatively short time, transformed it into a model city garden.

Mrs. Bowen—a garden consultant, and author of *Gardening in the City* —tested over three hundred plants before she selected the few that would give maximum beauty with minimum care.

A second goal was to provide an attractive outdoor living room. How well this was achieved may be judged from the photograph of the finished garden; note that it appears not only inviting but at least twice the size of its actual 25 × 42 feet. In this section the "yards" are divided from each other by high, ugly wooden fences so the first problem was to plant these out with high shrubs—including both broadleaved evergreens and flowering deciduous types—and vines, especially ivies. Evergreen bamboo, which flourishes under difficult conditions and forms a dense screen, was used.

The stepping-stone path through the lawn leads to a tiny oasis in the form of a rock-rimmed pool in the left rear corner. This layout, leading the eye, by means of the curving path, obliquely to the farther corner of the garden, successfully disguises the commonplace oblong shape of the plot.

60

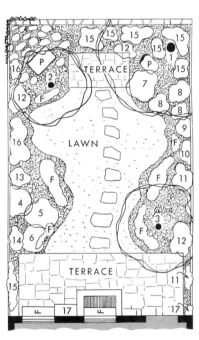

1   *Large Ailanthus*
2   *Flowering Crab*
3   *White Dogwood*
4   *White Rose of Sharon*
5   *Pyracantha*
6   *Azalea poukmensis*
7   *Azalea amoena*
8   *Pieris japonica*
9   *Weigela*
10   *Hardy Fig*
11   *Ilex crenata*
12   *Rhododendron maximum*
13   *Euonymus alatus*
14   *Flowering Almond*
15   *Bambusa Metake*
16   *Hardy Ferns*
17   *Virginia Creeper and Boston Ivy*

Broken sunlight, falling through the foliage of ailanthus, locust and other trees tolerant of city life, makes rhododendron shimmer and gives brilliance to blooming tulips. Wisteria hangs heavily purple against the buildings and fountain-like day lilies promise bloom to come.

Communal Haven

Shared by a group of owners
EAST SIXTY-FIFTH STREET, NEW YORK CITY

Oɴ ᴛʜᴇ facing page, a garden shutting out the crowded urban environment was attained, but the garden was small. In the planting shown here, several owners of adjoining property sacrificed the complete privacy of individual gardens, did away with fences, and created a much larger and more beautiful garden area that all could enjoy together.

Another modern adaptation of this idea is to be found in the current practice in many towns and suburban communities of eliminating line hedges and fences in front of and between houses. Thus the community shares a clear, open and airy stretch of lawn and shrubbery, with private areas concentrated to the rear of residences.

In this urban community garden a mass of spring color is achieved with tulips, azaleas, wisteria, dogwood and other spring-flowering shrubs, and the marble fountain with its sculptured figure lends a note of Old World remoteness and restfulness in keeping with the spirit of the whole.

61

All the warm colors of autumn meet in this outdoor living room, shaded by an oak tree and bounded by a country fence against which lilacs grow. The rosy brick terrace is a perfect foil for the dark red velvet chrysanthemums on both sides of the steps. Yellow and White Avalanche are interplanted with ageratum for a touch of blue, and low euonymus and spreading ivy form a ground cover which defies weeds.

Cycle of Seasons on Long Island

Mrs. Harry I. Nicholas

OYSTER BAY, LONG ISLAND

ONE of the chief objectives of modern gardening practice is to provide color from the first sunny days of spring until the killing frosts of late autumn. At this lovely home on Long Island's North Shore this end has been achieved to a remarkable degree.

The spring show starts with the earliest of bulbs, such as chionodoxas, crocuses and grape-hyacinths; continues through the daffodils and tulips, iris and Oriental poppies, delphinium, lilies, phlox and a host of annuals; and ends in the fall with a grand show of chrysanthemums.

The owner's chief problem was to keep the garden in scale with the house, which was formerly a gardener's cottage on the Nicholas estate. Nothing massive or very tall could be used, so it was necessary to depend principally on color. Low evergreens such as box for landscape effects and backgrounds have been utilized near the house.

Open fields, with low fences, give an attractive offscape to this garden and the house which it enhances. To maintain clear views of these rolling fields, the garden itself has been left open, with only a few shrubs (lilacs) and small trees (dogwoods) to break the horizontal fence lines.

The garden, set on two levels, is rectangular and thus in harmony with the fields that lie beyond, and even the flower beds follow the same pattern. To reduce even further the break between the garden and the surrounding fields, the flower beds are at some points carried beyond the fence, creating the illusion that the wealth of bloom is actually spilling over into the fields beyond. In these "extramural" beds only low-growing species, such as

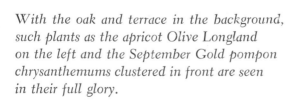

With the oak and terrace in the background, such plants as the apricot Olive Longland on the left and the September Gold pompon chrysanthemums clustered in front are seen in their full glory.

PHOTOS BY GOTTSCHO-SCHLEISNER (COURTESY OF *Flower Grower*)

mountain phlox, primulas, alyssum, false Solomon's seal and cerastium, are planted.

Petunias, zinnias, and dwarf bedding dahlias are grown or are "set in" to carry on until the big autumn display of chrysanthemums in variety takes over.

Maintaining the continuous succession of bloom achieved in this garden is no small undertaking, especially where—as here—the owner does not have a staff of trained gardeners to assist her.

In addition to the large replacements of annuals set in after the spring bulb show is over, Mrs. Nicholas accomplishes this through the use of such long-blooming perennials as huechera and dianthus, through heliotrope and lantana, which give color from midsummer to frost, and through the Dr. Van Fleet and Golden Climber roses, which rebloom freely in autumn.

Glistening white arabis and iberis, blue pulmonaria, myosotis, wood phlox, violas and Alyssum saxatile overflow the fence in this low spring border. The drooping jewel-like blossoms against the fence at the right are Solomon's-seal.

This year-round garden is distinctive in that maintenance, for an area so large and with such a generous variety in plant material, has been cut to a minimum. There are no flower borders to require constant replanting and weeding and no difficult trimming along paths and edges. Where such architectural forms as globes, pyramids and the like are used, the designer has employed such plants as White Pine, Mugho Pine and box, which tend to assume these shapes with a minimum of shearing.

A Triumph of Naturalistic Modern

Mr. and Mrs. Umberto Innocenti

ROSLYN, LONG ISLAND, N.Y.

IN MANY ways this delightful garden represents a triumph of modern landscape design for the moderate-sized estate. This is not surprising, for it is the home of one of America's leading landscape architects, and embodies the principles that he has evolved from a lifetime of work in his chosen field.

This garden is not done in what would ordinarily be called the modern style, but a glance at any of the accompanying photographs will indicate third-dimensional design in mass and texture achieved not with architectural materials, art forms or topiary work, but by the skillful use of natural plant forms such as Mugho Pines and various other low-growing evergreens.

It is noticeable, too, that these borders are artfully "faced down"—much in the manner of the typical wide perennial borders in English gardens—so that no plants hide or interfere with those behind them. Most of the trees—of which there are many species—used here and there as accent points, are trimmed high so that other plants may be successfully grown beneath them.

Although deciduous trees, evergreens (many of them dwarf or spreading types), and shrubs constitute in the main the plant materials utilized, color is not lacking. Flowering shrubs, both as individual specimens and—as in the case of azaleas and rhododendrons—in masses, provide breathtaking color early in the season. Perennials and annuals are employed for effective color accents rather than in the usual crowded beds or borders.

The beauty of marginal plantings is enhanced by uncluttered open sweeps of lawn which make

65

New England Heritage

Dr. and Mrs. George C. Shattuck and Mr. Henry L. Shattuck

BROOKLINE, MASSACHUSETTS

Viewed from above, the formal design of this box-enclosed flower garden is evident. The tree in the center is a pyramidal juniper.

Here, fortunately, we have preserved, with comparatively few changes, an estate dating back to 1800. In fact, work was begun on the development of the property ten or fifteen years before that.

The original owner, Colonel Thomas Handasyd Perkins, whose fortune was made in the China trade, purchased a large tract of land in Brookline in 1779. The present estate, which is part of that land, has remained in the hands of direct descendants. Many of the original features of the place, such as extensive greenhouses, have disappeared or have been replaced. The last of Colonel Perkins' grape-houses, taken down in 1933, was still heated with old smoke-flues built of brick. A "billiard house" and a "pheasant run" are long since gone.

But the high brick walls and many of the original trees remain. At the foot of the garden there is, still in good repair, a brick building that in Colonel Perkins' time housed apprentice gardeners and was called "the college." In the period from 1885 to 1909 the Colonel's granddaughter and her husband, Mr. and Mrs. Henry Lee, added arborvitae hedges, a box garden, a pergola, a pleached allée with European hornbeam and a rockery surmounted by an Italian summer house. These features remain, the pleached allée being of special interest.

This estate provides a good example of the impact such places have had upon horticulture in America, the records of the Massachusetts Horticultural Society being studded with references to its contributions. As early as 1832 the president of the Society declared: "Colonel Perkins has made great successful efforts to advance the culture of choice fruits, as well as to encourage a taste for ornamental gardening, as is well known by those who have visited his beautiful grounds. From . . . all parts of the world he has been enabled to collect numerous rare and valuable trees and plants; and with that liberality for which he is distinguished he has freely distributed them throughout the country. Such munificent patrons . . . not only accelerate the progress of horticulture in their immediate vicinity, but the influence of their practical operations is extended over the Republic, and will be gratefully remembered by their fellow citizens."

Here, the hard curve of the driveway is softened by the trees at the right. In the foreground stands a young oak and box, and at left a group of junipers.

68

Among the "rare" plants mentioned in an article in *The American Gardener's Magazine* in 1836 are *Enkianthus quinqueflora, Strelitzia augusta, Salvia fulgens* and *S. splendens*, and *Acacia longifolia*. Referring to ericas grown by the head gardener for Colonel Perkins, an interesting comment was: "Notwithstanding the opinion of some intelligent gardeners that heaths cannot be grown with success in our climate, we never saw any look more flourishingly." Another of this gardener's specialties was the raising of camellias from seed.

After Colonel Perkins' death in 1854 at the age of ninety years, the estate passed to his daughter, Mrs. Samuel Cabot (Eliza Perkins); in 1885 it passed to her daughter Mrs. Henry Lee (Elizabeth Cabot); Mrs. Frederick C. Shattuck (Elizabeth Lee) inherited it in 1910, and in 1931 her sons, Dr. George C. and Mr. Henry L. Shattuck became the owners.

Of the garden today, Dr. Shattuck feels that its outstanding features are its Old World flavor, and a unique quality that is not easy to describe but is largely the graciousness that mellow age lends to its many fine features. The wealth of flowering shrubs that bloom in sequence through April, May and June include forsythia, cornus, mahonia, an extensive collection of rhododendrons and azaleas; kalmia, andromeda (*Pieris japonica*), redbud and many varieties of crab apples, apples, cherries, plums and, of course, lilacs. The fine display of autumn foliage and a wealth of evergreens in winter give it year-round beauty.

In 1954 this garden was awarded the coveted H. H. Hunnewell Medal of the Massachusetts Horticultural Society.

Above: *Hybrid rhododendrons soften this long, straight garden walk. Perennials are planted along the old brick wall. Farther back, on the right, are fine arborvitae specimens, and beyond them stretches a sheared arborvitae hedge.*

Below, left to right: *Three of the fine old trees for which the estate is famous: an Umbrella Pine, a White Pine and a beech.*

On this hillside of laurel the blue water of Long Island Sound is framed by oaks and evergreens such as the groups of Blue Spruce and Mugho Pine near center right. Along the grass path floribunda roses ramble and one clump of lavender brings the color of the sea into the garden itself.

Seaside Garden with a Difference

Mrs. Harold P. Whitmore

GREENWICH, CONNECTICUT

ALTHOUGH perhaps not a garden in the usual sense of the term, this is a most interesting piece of landscaping. It is a planted waterside slope, gradual in some places and steep in others, which has been left, on the whole, as nature molded it.

Much of such original native material as existed has been preserved. Introduced plants, with few exceptions, have been those that are indigenous to the area—such as the mountain laurel, white pine, and junipers—or at least relatives thereof. The result is a wholly charming, naturalistic scene which gives one much the feeling of rambling through a glorified New England hillside pasture that happens to slope down headlong to the boat-studded blue waters of Long Island Sound.

Here and there are outcroppings of rock, some of them offering precarious footing above the water. Wandering paths lead the visitor to ever-changing views of both the terrain roundabout and the irregular shoreline below.

This apparently haphazard, but actually very carefully managed, planting differs widely from the usual seaside estate garden. It is evidence that in landscaping, as in other forms of artistic design, there can be no rigid standards. In its refreshing originality it suggests the value of embracing the opportunities presented by a unique garden site, of making the most of natural contours and native materials instead of converting them to a conventional design.

Remade from an old New England farm the beautiful simplicity of the original lingers in this spring scene. Peaches and cherries are already in magnificent bloom while great elms and oaks, not yet in leaf, are outlined against the sky. Forsythia in the background repeats the yellow of the house walls.

Around a New England Pond

Mrs. Arthur Adams

DOVER, MASSACHUSETTS

When this garden was begun in 1917, it was a typical abandoned New England farm. Over the years it has been gradually converted into an unusual and charming estate. The landscaping was originally planned by Guy H. Lee, but it was never carried out in detail. Changes were made as they suggested themselves and as opportunity offered. The new owners found that what they wanted most was a pleasant and serene view and a garden adapted to comfortable living—one that would require neither too much expense in the making nor too great effort in maintenance. Securing privacy was not a problem since the property was of sufficient extent to assure this.

They began with the pond. When it became evident that it would form the central theme of the garden, the land between it and the house was graded to a gentle slope and a low stone retaining wall built around the pond. Above and below this, flower beds were put in and planted with bulbs for spring color and with perennials for summer and fall. Then followed the creation of a naturalistic walk through the woods around the edge of the pond. Here the low, moist ground made a natural home for many kinds of wildflowers. Eventually, however, the leading role in this section of the landscaping went to an extensive planting of *Primula japonica* which started with a trowelful of tiny primula seedlings given by a friend.

Not all of this charming place is in the naturalistic style, however, for another project was a very adequate fruit garden, bordered with apples and pears espaliered in various designs, and—as a focal point—a small, circular garden house made entirely of espaliered apples. A fine collection of lilacs and other flowering shrubs is featured elsewhere.

71

Accent on the Natural

Mr. and Mrs. Robert W. Stoddard
WORCESTER, MASSACHUSETTS

On the right is an extraordinary wall of Maidenhair Fern stretching under evergreen and deciduous trees as far as the eye can see. Edged with Vinca minor *and Creeping Euonymus, it forms a cool, damp corridor of green, delightful in hot weather. On the left,* Bergenia cordifolia *and gray Japanese Ferns look out from beneath Maxwell Spruces and other evergreen shrubs.*

BUILT within the last decade, this estate is an illuminating example of the way most modern landscape architects have abandoned the formal "laid out" designs of a generation or two ago.

Here it was the considered purpose of the owners to keep away from any obvious appearance of landscaping; to preserve to the fullest extent the natural beauty of the terrain; and to avoid any planting scheme which would reveal where the work of man left off and that of nature began. In carrying out this general scheme they had the co-operation of an architect whose aim is to model in masses in order to avoid having details distract from the total effect.

The chief objective here was a garden and grounds that would provide the maximum in recreation and enjoyment, and this purpose ruled out at the start the usual type of estate garden. Since the place was densely wooded and the topography uneven, a variety of problems presented themselves. The land drops off at the rear, and slopes up a hill at the north, the rise affording natural protection. A great deal of grading had to be done around the residence. To maintain a natural ap-

Looking across this wide, sloping lawn, one sees the rose garden as it appears in June with its protective background of clustering trees. At the far left, behind the roses, a magnificent laurel bush is a mass of blossom.

pearance, many small slopes, contours, banks and planted walls were carefully blended and any suggestion of a large overall grade—a common tendency in grading—was avoided. The sculptured curves and rolling contours in the extensive lawn, most of which is in fairly dense but "high" shade, are particularly effective in this respect.

In the selection and placing of plant material, three objectives were kept in mind. The first was to avoid the use of exotic—or even exotic-looking —subjects. The second was to avoid small, spotty plantings, but rather to employ large groups or even sweeping masses—as nature usually does; and the third was to maintain a certain amount of overall bloom from melting snows to late fall, rather than a series of special displays for spring, summer and autumn.

In opening up the woods to obtain vistas and off-views, great care was exercised to save and to display to the best advantage the beautiful natural

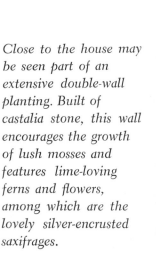

Close to the house may be seen part of an extensive double-wall planting. Built of castalia stone, this wall encourages the growth of lush mosses and features lime-loving ferns and flowers, among which are the lovely silver-encrusted saxifrages.

PHOTOS BY MARVIN RICHMOND

stands of mountain laurel and the fine specimens of juniper. In many instances, too, exciting colonies of wildflowers were encouraged to develop and spread. Where wildlings were brought in, they were carefully selected for compatibility, not only in culture but also in color and character, with native material.

There are several features of the place which

maidenhair, a rather rare, light green, lacy species, with wiry, dark stems, usually found only in small, isolated colonies.

Another feature is a long, double wall, constructed to look like a retaining wall, built of gray, porous limestone (castalia stone), along the rear of the house, with steps at one end. Castalia stone is conducive to the lush growth of some mosses

Here a close-up autumnal view of the rose garden shows clearly the long pearl-gray bank of the tapered border of Festuca glauca, *a decorative grass, mulched in blue stone. Still young and sparse as seen in the photographs on the preceding page, it is here well established. Planted at the top of a dry wall it makes a silvery contrast to the adjoining border of perennial flowers.*

the owners find especially satisfactory. The most famous of these is the Maidenhair Fern glen. The owners point out that one of their original desires was a bank "dripping with maidenhair." To achieve this, a deep cut was made in one side of the garden to form a utility path to a lower level. One side of this was then built up, with field stones laid in loam, into a sloping retaining wall. Maidenhair and polypodium ferns were planted between the stones. The result, after a few seasons' growth, was what appears to be a solid wall of

and of lime-loving ferns and flowers. An extensive wall planting of these, together with the frosty-looking, encrusted silver saxifrages (*S. crustata*), contributes an effect that is both unusual and charming.

Still another interesting bit of planting is a long, tapering strip of pearl-gray grass (*Festuca glauca*), mulched with crushed bluestone, at the top of a curving dry wall bordering a perennial bed. The gray-foliaged Japanese fern is another plant which has been utilized as a "blender" in this garden.

74

PHOTOS BY MARVIN RICHMOND

*The rose garden in autumn is enhanced by the tapestry-like foliage of
the surrounding trees.*

Carved out of rugged terrain is a remarkably serene and almost cloistered area leading up to a shrinelike teahouse. Contributing to the effect is English ivy in the foreground, a line of maples at the right, a semiformal group of evergreens, including arborvitae and junipers, around the teahouse, and White Pine and other evergreens in the background.

Baroque in the Berkshire Hills

Miss Mabel Choate STOCKBRIDGE, MASSACHUSETTS

THIS remarkable garden in the foothills of western Massachusetts has been under more or less continuous development for seventy years. Thus it shows the cumulative impact of all the landscape styles that have swept over the country in this period. Yet—thanks to the two landscape architects,

Nathan Bartlett who first laid out the garden in 1885, and Fletcher Steele who took charge of it in 1926—it has been welded into an original and most appealing unity. Few gardens in America have lasted so long or survived so well.

The problem in the beginning was a double one.

The view from the walled courtyard is framed by tall, matched firs. Within the walls, Oriental simplicity reigns: a few plants in pots, such as the geraniums at the edge of the terrace, a flowering shrub or two, dwarf fruit trees pruned low, and stone dragons that in the Orient might guard against wandering warriors and ragged beggars.

The first objective was to exploit a variety of fine views from a very uneven terrain—there is a steep drop of a hundred feet or more from the house site to that of the stables; and secondly, to provide enough level areas from which these views could be restfully and securely enjoyed. The house itself and the original landscaping itself was a good example of the transition period between the formal estate in the European manner and the freer, more open approach in America.

When Mr. Steele took over, his aim was to keep, where possible, the best of the original design and at the same time to remodel the garden in order to bring it more into harmony with a newer house which had been erected subsequently. Since the house was on a rather palatial scale and showed a strong Oriental influence, this was no simple matter: such a design does not automatically fit a New England hilltop.

That Mr. Steele succeeded is apparent from the photographs shown here; how he did so requires a little explanation. In the first place, his style is quite free. Although he employed Oriental elements, these are not Oriental gardens. The manipulation of the grades is, if anything, baroque, as in the grass slope (top, right) with its metal-edged inserts of gravel. Some elements are almost Venetian in their playfulness (see the water garden, page 165). At the same time, his combination of highly formal elements, like the Chinese teahouse and terrace, with informal plantings and rolling lawns is more in the English tradition.

Today, of course, the Choate gardens also have the kind of magnificent plant specimens which come only with time and care. The vistas laid out so many years ago are now framed in towering conifers and massive deciduous trees, the lawns are velvet smooth, the walls mossy. Yet, for all its air of lushness, this is a garden of comparatively easy maintenance. All the plant material is hardy; none of it fussy or demanding of special cultivation. Instead of fragile flowering material, attention is focused on form, pattern and texture. How this simplifies maintenance is evident from the fact that all "gardening" is done by farm hands under the direction of the farm superintendent.

PAUL E. GENEREUX

PAUL E. GENEREUX

Top: *The secluded, Oriental atmosphere is illustrated in the way the terrace flows downward in a spreading series of shallow, cut stone stairs and onto a wide, sloping turf area dominated by striking gravel scrolls. The lines of the scrolls* (top) *and of the terrace* (middle) *are broken by such plantings as dwarf roses, a fig tree in a tub, and a tree peony; and the Oriental feeling of the architecture of the Moon Gate Garden* (bottom) *is carried out in exotic plants such as Elephant Ears* (Colocasia esculenta).

ARTHUR C. HASKELL

Fieldstone
and
Autumn
Color

Mr. and Mrs.
Charles Burlingham

WILTON, CONN.

GOTTSCHO-SCHLEISNER (COURTESY OF *Flower Grower*)

*The retaining walls of native stone lend a rugged beauty to this
Connecticut garden. Curved beds, backed by trimmed arborvitae and edged
with box, are planted for spring and autumn show. Bulbs are featured
in spring. In autumn, the colors of recent varieties of such large-flowered
chrysanthemums as Huntsman, Magnolia, Lavender Lady and Bronze
Pyramid vie with the rich tapestry of the surrounding trees.*

Along a New England Roadside

Mrs. Joseph M. Batchelder

PEACH'S POINT, MASSACHUSETTS

WHEN the present owner took over this little garden in 1951, the steeply sloping area between the house and the road was the site of a stony brook which served as an open town drain. A dense growth of chokecherry and witchgrass only partially concealed an accumulation of tin cans, broken bottles and similar debris. By dint of much labor the new owner cleaned out the plot, rearranged some of the rocks and put in a path of flat stepping stones along the course of the brook.

The planting which followed was designed—without benefit of any professional advice—to make, in the words of Mrs. Batchelder, "a maximum spring show with a minimum of care during the summer months." For the owner spends practically all of her spare time in summer on the water, and the garden therefore gets little attention from June to September. Evergreens of various sizes and textures provide a pleasing winter design.

The plant materials used are the simplest and most easily cared for —as a glance at the plan below indicates. A great variety of spring bulbs, supplemented by such spring-flowering perennials as primulas, forget-me-nots, violets and dwarf iris, in irregular drifts and masses that give them a completely natural appearance, supply a wealth of color and charm. Though this garden seems to be in an enchanted world of its own, it is, in reality, right by the side of the road and can be enjoyed by every passerby.

Above: *Moisture-loving primulas compete with iberis, white daffodils, grape hyacinths, epimedium and yellow lady-slippers in this stream-side spring paradise.*

Below: *The stream itself with its rocky bed and its border planting of myosotis, narcissus, primulas, pansies, violas, hostas and dwarf iris.*

PHOTOS BY PAUL E. GENEREUX

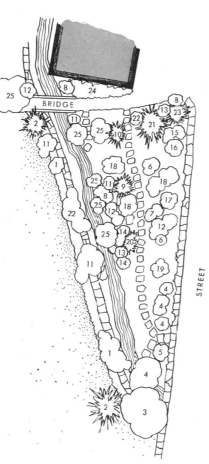

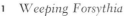

1   *Weeping Forsythia*
2 and 3   *Hemlock*
4   *Mayflower Viburnum*
5   *Azalea hinodegiri*
6   *Korean Azalea*
7   *Carolina Rhododendron*
8   *Winter-creeper Euonymus*
9   *Arborvitae*
10   *Chamaecyparis*
11   *Leucothoe*
12   *Mountain Laurel*
13   *Pieris*
14   *Hybrid Azalea*
15   *Rhododendron Amoenum*
16   *Gray Birch*
17   *White Dogwood*
18   *Hybrid Rhododendrons*
19   *Golden Weeping Willow*
20   *Juniper*
21   *Austrian Pine*
22   *Rose Daphne*
23   *Hatfield Yew*
24   *Myrtle, Dwarf Veronica, Violets*
25   *Elm*

Garden of Many Facets

"Morelands"

Mr. and Mrs. Frederick F. Brewster

DUBLIN, NEW HAMPSHIRE

MAKING a striking contrast to the fine example of a small garden on the preceding page is Morelands, one of the most famous of New England's larger gardens. Morelands, in fact, is annually visited by many horticultural enthusiasts.

Unlike the Batchelder garden, however, this garden—or more accurately gardens, for there is a series of them—has been carefully planned to provide continuous color from spring to frost, with special emphasis on the four summer months. Spring arrives late, and winter early, at this 1,500-foot elevation with its sustained subzero weather.

Originally an old farm of 850 acres, Morelands had long been neglected when it was purchased by the Brewsters at public auction in 1925. Much of the property was heavily timbered, including a large sugar bush that supplied maple sugar; the land adjacent to the residence and the dairy buildings had been used for hayfields and the growing of potatoes and corn. Such planting as had been done was beyond reclaiming, since the residence had been unoccupied for years. The new owners did, however, inherit many fine trees—oaks, birch, pines (Austrian, Scotch, and Red, as well as the native White), spruce, hemlock and fir, native elms, and a rare specimen of the superb English Elm. Above all, they had a grand view of Dublin lake, with majestic Mount Monadnock beyond.

The original main house was built about 1888. Like most New England homes it was of wood construction—clapboards and shingles—architecturally very different from the mansions on the big southern estates, where the problem was to keep out sun and heat, rather than cold.

The first landscaping was undertaken in 1926, with an architect's plans that included a terrace facing the lake and a walled garden featuring the English Elm. During the next two years the rock garden was constructed and planted, and in 1930 the series of little individual gardens, each more or less complete in itself but related to the others. The gently sloping land was adapted to this treatment, for each garden could be placed on a different level and enclosed by a hedge; but the series was united by a long mall from the walled garden to the "pleasance" or shaded pleasure garden, with its wall fountain backed by a Concolor Fir on an axis with the English Elm in the terrace garden.

The series of individual gardens, each distinct in design and planting, includes the following:

A rock garden that is profusely planted with alpine rock-loving plants, and suitable perennials

This "sanctuary garden," surrounded by pines and hemlocks, is graced by a statue of St. Francis and a shallow basin of running water. It is planted with mahonia, andromeda, Maidenhair and Dagger Ferns, and everbearing strawberries.

and annuals to provide continuous bloom to be enjoyed from spring to frost, with clipped ornamental hemlocks and yews as accents. Sheltering clipped yews enclose a bird-bath, with ferns, violets and forget-me-nots covering much of the flagstone.

An English sunken garden that is entered through a hedge of sheared arborvitae. Sheared retinosporas form the sides, and sheared Canadian Hemlock the oval end. Four elevated beds are edged with stone copings, and contain standard heliotropes (variety Edith Dennison) above mass plantings of Heliotrope Royal Fragrance.

A French garden that is enclosed by a hedge of sheared arborvitae, cut to different heights to coincide with the different levels. It includes two long, narrow, elevated beds with stone copings, planted with standard fuchsias (variety Marshall) over Pink Pearl Begonias, and edged with White Gem Sweet Alyssum. At the end is a shallow, circular pool with a single *jet d'eau* in front of a double taxus hedge, clipped to different levels, with stone steps at either side leading to a semicircular terrace supporting four Louis XV stone figures.

A waterfall and white garden hedged with clipped hemlock, accented by specimen arborvitae. At the base of the pool, stone steps, bordered with violets, forget-me-nots, Japanese Iris, hosta and columbine, lead to a primrose path. The note of white is maintained by elevated semicircular beds devoted to *Lilium candidum* and standard white lantanas, above a ground cover of *Vinca minor alba* and Begonia Snowbank. Lead figures of dancing girls, on stone bases, divide the garden. Here there is a vista to the pool garden, which is enclosed by double hedges of sheared Canadian Hemlock, one considerably higher than the other. Four circular, elevated beds, edged with bluestone, are separated by stone benches and planted with Hybrid Tuberous Begonias. The pool, edged with Hand's Ivy, has at its center a small fountain ornament—a boy with a turtle on his back. From here there is a vista to the waterfall garden.

Finally there is the Sanctuary, entered by a pine-needle-covered, fern-bordered path. Here the planting—informally arranged in contrast to that of the other gardens—includes mahonia, ferns, digitalis and everbearing strawberries.

Above: *The hedge-enclosed English garden is bordered by beds of heliotropes with standard heliotropes set in.*

Above: *The terrace is walled at the far end with sheared hemlock and bordered by box and sheared White Pine. The topiary garden is shown below.*

Cascade
of
Color

Mrs. Dacre Bush

CAPE NEDDICK, MAINE

*The vivid blue of delphiniums dominates this
Maine garden. Also featured are masses of pink,
rose and white phlox against a wall of pines.*

NEW ENGLAND coastal areas have long been famous for the extra brilliance of color that annuals and perennials acquire in summer and early autumn gardens there. Typical in this respect is this pine-sheltered hillside garden where phlox, poppies, asters, petunias and a host of other familiar flowers tumble downhill in a torrent of color to meet their own reflections in a stone-bordered, mirror-smooth pool.

Spring comes late along this part of the coast and in many gardens there is little or no attempt to procure any marked display of early bloom. When the brief summer does arrive, however, moist nights and days that are not too hot make up for the reluctant spring. Protection from offshore winds, essential in this area, is often provided by nature in the form of dense groves of shore pines that act as a windbreak.

82

In the French Manner

Mr. and Mrs. Ernest Kanzler
DETROIT, MICHIGAN

Tulips, flowering crabs, redbud and cherries tightly frame this turf panel and its terminal statue.

Like many of the gardens in the Grosse Point district, this one was laid out before World War I by the famous midwestern landscape architect, Miss Ellen Shipman. A strict traditionalist, she favored formal and French designs, intended more to be looked at than lived in. Because land in suburban areas is much scarcer and skilled garden labor all but nonexistent today, such gardens are becoming rarer with each passing season.

Yet designs of this sort, especially when they have been well cared for over the decades, can be both impressive and satisfying. This is especially true in the Great Lakes region, where the blooming season is relatively short and much reliance must be placed on form and structure if the garden is to be attractive around the year. These conditions do not imply, of course, that such gardens cannot have flowers; on the contrary, as these pictures show, the Kanzler garden has herbaceous borders for continuous summer bloom. And this color is handsomely reinforced in spring by flowering shrubs and trees.

A principal feature of the grounds is a large *tapis vert,* smooth and green as a parlor carpet, which runs east from the house to the lake (above). It is outlined with flowering borders which are backed in turn by flowering crabs, dogwood and redbud. For later bloom there are standard wisterias and lilacs trimmed in tree form to single stems. Another typical feature of gardens of this genre is the use of a sculpture (left) which acts as a terminus to a vista from the house.

Pink rhododendron and tulips with a carpet of Grape Hyacinth Heavenly Blue surround a piece of Louis XV statuary.

Summer Garden
in the
North Woods

Mr. and Mrs. John Sargent Pillsbury
LAKE MINNETONKA, MINNESOTA

Year-round gardening in the far north presents many special problems. The growing season is short and the dormant period long, with a heavy snow cover concealing the garden design and deep frost immobilizing the plants. But a garden for a summer home, like this one in the lake district of northern Minnesota, is in many ways a much simpler matter. For then the period of use coincides with the growing season; and this season is itself almost ideal, without either the extreme heat or the droughts that plague the gardener farther south.

Above: *An inviting grass path, bordered by such perennials as day lilies and by low annuals, leads through a grove of trees and shrubs to the lake beyond.*

Right: *The wide and tranquil expanse of the lake has been made an integral part of the landscape. The velvety lawn is bordered with petunias and other annuals and enclosed by vine-covered walls and sheared hedges kept low.*

The Pillsbury summer home is an old and well-established place on the shores of Lake Minnetonka near Crystal Bay. It dates from a generous epoch when even summer homes were developed at the estate scale, and is premised on professional gardeners. In addition to broad expanses of lawn and woodland, it has a series of specialized gardens: a terrace garden and a long, formal *allée* adjoining the house; a cutting garden of both perennials and annuals; a vegetable garden. But though it has most of the features of an estate in the grand manner, it is pleasantly free from pretension and thus seems especially well suited to the casual summer life of such a region.

Ivied walls and formal treatment lend this summer home the dignity of a year-round residence.

Pattern for a Georgian House

Mrs. Roy D. Chapin

GROSSE POINT FARMS, MICHIGAN

THE wide use of the formal garden—whether English, Italian or French in derivation—came to an end in the early 1930's, along with the general decline of estate construction. But this type of design, although frankly derivative, has certain functional advantages, especially in the Middle West. Here, where the winters are long and hard, the season of leaf and flower is relatively short. The architectural garden, with its permanent form and structure, is relatively independent of such climatic factors and consequently preserves its designed appearance around the year.

The Chapin estate fits perfectly into this category. Its gardens are architectural in design and feeling. Each main view from the house is terminated with an architectural feature; each of the areas is enclosed like a room, excluding the outside world. Terraces, flower beds, and pools are rectilinear in outline. They are separated from each other by brick walls, trimmed hedges or ornamental fencing of grilles and gates. Where vistas occur, they are like doors in a room, framed by symmetrical trees or plants. Even the paved areas carry out this geometry of design in size, shape and color.

The box-edged formal beds on this handsome flagstone terrace are solidly filled with wax begonias in various colors. A fine terra cotta jar is planted with miniature ivy, and ivies and euonymus climb the enclosing balustrade. The hedge at the extreme left is clipped ilex.

The plant material is used in such a way as to contribute to this overall design, being massed for effect rather than displayed as individual units. Predominant are rhododendrons, azaleas and kalmias, with junipers, ilex and hollies for the clipped hedges. These are interplanted with bulbs for seasonal color—tulips, iris and lilies. Elsewhere there is a low border of rock plants—leucojum, iberis, creeping phlox, fritillarias, dianthus and alpine daffodils; but even these are handled in a rather formal manner.

Though the terrain is fairly level, the gardens have more topographic variety than may appear from the photographs. The lawn around the house flows down to a second level and fans out in a wide area at the back. On the entrance front it runs down through a clipped *allée* to a still lower open area beyond.

Left: *The lily pool is fed by an antique fountain mounted against a brick arch in the towering wall. The ancient pillared marble arch in the foreground adds to the nostalgic atmosphere.*

Right: *The house terraces are enclosed by brick walls with marble copings and piers surmounted by bronze cocks.*

PHOTOS BY KONSTANTIN J. KOSTICH

In the Italian Tradition

Mrs. William G. Mather

CLEVELAND, OHIO

Above: *The rectangular lily pool with its
central statue is one hedge-enclosed portion of
the large Italian garden on this estate. Great
hydrangeas in metal urns are set around its edge.*

Below: *A massive Italian antique fountain is set
in a green wild garden of rhododendron,
ivies, lily-of-the-valley, ferns and other
plants that can thrive in the shade of tall
elms and spreading beeches.*

THESE gardens are in a large and well-established estate on the shores of Lake Erie. Designed in the traditional Italian manner and on the grand scale so popular a quarter of a century ago, they represent today the results of long and continuous attention. They embrace a number of specialized gardens, including the two shown here. The owner describes the wild garden as "a laboratory for the study of shade plants . . . ivy, Christmas-rose, lilies-of-the-valley, ginger root, violets, Lady and Christmas Fern, Leather Woodfern and Snow Thoroughwort." Rhododendrons from England and South Carolina form a complete border around the area, and the canopy of elm and beech trees provides the light shade necessary for the plants.

The Italian garden, another feature of the place, is strictly axial in design. It terminates at one end with a pergola furnished with Old World marbles, Persian tiles, ceramic tubs and comfortable furniture. At the other end is a teahouse which serves as a foyer to a series of greenhouses in which are grown espaliered nectarines, peaches and grapes. There are also an orchid house and houses for the ornamental plants with which the garden proper is "furnished" in summer: heliotrope, lantana, verbena, fuchsia, and so forth—all trained to standard tree form.

PHOTOS BY KONSTANTIN J. KOSTICH

Water Lily Garden in Missouri

Mr. and Mrs. Harris Armstrong
KIRKWOOD, MISSOURI

WHEN architect Harris Armstrong built this combination guest house and studio on the grounds of his suburban home, he located it astraddle a small, spring-fed brook. First he dammed the brook, creating a little pond, carefully modeling the contours of its banks, and then fashioning a small egg-shaped island. The building itself, as light and gay as a Japanese teahouse, is served by a little bridge and sheltered catwalk.

The pond is planted with lotus and various water lilies, native and exotic, day- and night-blooming. To prevent erosion, avoid marshy margins and simplify maintenance the entire pond is edged with a metal strip set in concrete. The lawn and graveled surfaces are flush with the top of this metal curbing, thus preserving the crisp outline of the pond. The planting, kept sparse and simple, is largely yew, cotoneaster, pine and cypress.

A metal curbing, embedded in concealed concrete, gives this little pond garden a clear, crisp edge. The only blooming plants are the water lilies: native and tropical, day- and night-blooming, and including the African Victoria Regina and Egyptian lotus.

HEDRICH-BLESSING

*The classic elements of the English garden—roses and perennials—are
combined with taste and imagination in this Midwestern estate. Despite
the large scale of boxwood and shrubs, this is a relatively recent garden.*

Pattern in Flowing Lines

Mrs. Chester F. Kroger

CINCINNATI, OHIO

ORIGINALLY this garden—then very much smaller—was devoted only to perennials. When the owner decided to add a rose garden and a herb garden, the problem was where and how to place these without creating a chopped-up effect. The solution was to sacrifice a few trees, and re-grade and extend the existing garden in both directions, thus securing a unified, long vista from a terrace above the rose garden.

On the upper level, beds were established along the sloped walk leading down to the lower level. In these beds color is maintained throughout the season: light blue pansies in early spring are followed by white petunias and purple torenias, and these in turn by dwarf chrysanthemums that flower from late summer until heavy frosts.

Another specialty here is daffodils. A suitable setting for these was created by establishing a bit of woodland near the house. Here wildflowers in variety have been planted, care being exercised, however, to include only those holding their foliage throughout the summer, such as ferns, *Phlox divaricata* and *pulmonaria*. Such broadleaved evergreens as *Magnolia grandiflora,* ilex and azaleas have been used for their summer foliage.

The flowing lines of the landscape design as a whole, most of which can be glimpsed from the house terrace, are most satisfying. They present an ever-fresh view of the contrast between the strongly accented design of the rose garden on the intermediate level, the brilliant colors of the flower borders, and the muted greens of the herb garden.

89

Garden in the Heart
of the House

Mr. and Mrs. Richard Davis
MINNEAPOLIS, MINNESOTA

This patio in Minnesota is made possible by a glass roof. With the principal rooms all opening onto it through sliding glass walls, it gives a remarkable sense of greenery and space.

Though it is always summery in the patio, the rooms which face it also have glass walls toward the out-of-doors. In the long winters of the north, this makes for a series of exciting contrasts.

For people who live in the far north, the pleasures of the garden are ordinarily brief. Long, hard winters truncate a growing season which, while it lasts, is delightful. In a climate like that of Minneapolis, the problem for garden lovers is how to stay alive, so to speak, from one season to the next. The Davis house in Minneapolis gives a charming answer: for, in addition to a normal complement of handsomely landscaped grounds outside, it has a little glass-roofed garden at its heart. This enclosure is not very large but it does not have to be: a plashing fountain, some tubbed bay trees and a few potted flowering plants can, in midwinter, give a wonderful imitation of spring. Moreover, with its four glass walls opening into the main living areas of the house, the design creates an almost tropic sense of space, light and air.

A patio like this is actually a combination of the conservatory of fifty years ago and the *atrium* of the old Roman houses of Pompeii and Herculaneum. Like the former it is a cold-weather pleasure; but like the latter it is designed as the visual center of the house and not—as was true of many conservatories—a mere addition where few people ever went. The skylight is concealed, and the sunlight effectively dispersed, by a deep egg-crate ceiling. Lighting is concealed in these louvers so that the patio is a luminous center of interest day and night. Since the planting is all potted, the scheme can be varied at will—in fact, the owners have already altered the design shown here.

Garden rooms like this are not inexpensive: but for the gardener who lives in a climate where winters are long and severe it might well pay to allot a portion of the gardening budget to such a feature as this. It yields rich dividends during all those months when the outside garden is frozen and dead.

The only fixed elements are the pool with its plashing jet of water and the raked gravel floor. Plant material is all potted, which makes for easy maintenance and permits flexibility in changing color, texture or design.

This circular rose garden is planted around a central area of turf and stepping stones which was originally a cattle pond.

Garden for a Rugged Climate

Mr. and Mrs. Howard B. Peabody
LAKE FOREST, ILLINOIS

THIS is another example of a comparatively old garden (it was begun in 1928) that has been continuously developed under the loving care of the same owners from the beginning. Seeing the lush foliage today, it is hard to believe that this began as a Midwestern cow pasture with not a single tree or shrub on the place. According to Mrs. Peabody, there were only two points of any interest on the 3½-acre tract: the cattle pond and a natural ravine. The former she converted into the rose garden shown above. The latter was developed into a most successful rock garden built of "imported" stone—a carload of river-bottom limestone brought down from Wisconsin.

As it stands today, the Peabody place consists of not one but many gardens, all of them enclosed in trees and shrubbery which, by themselves, represent a victory over the difficult climate of the Lake Forest region. This is not a layout designed for grand vistas that can be picked up at a glance. It is more like a house made up of garden rooms that have to be walked through to be seen. The owners' objective was "bloom from earliest spring through to the first hard freeze in late fall." To achieve this, the planting was organized into a spring garden, a June garden, a midsummer and a fall garden. At a more utilitarian level, there is also a cutting garden, a vegetable plot and a bearing orchard. And all of these are laid out so as to create a sense of great space, full of peaceful prospects and secluded spots, despite the comparatively small tract of land.

The wise use of evergreens and flowering shrubs is largely responsible for the effect achieved. By enclosing each small garden in this way, not only is a lush background of green provided for the colorful flower beds and borders but protective walls of verdure are raised against prevailing winds and bitter cold.

In this intimate corner of the Peabody garden a curving path of massive river-bottom limestones from Wisconsin is bordered—and in places partly overrun—by creeping phlox, Alyssum saxatile citrinum and myosotis. Beyond, a flowering plum, the exquisite blossoms set off by a dark hemlock in the background, stands in front of a low dry stone wall planted with vines.

R. H. ANDERSON : F.P.G.

*Here the East, so far as plant material is concerned, has invaded the West.
Shrub roses, Harrison's Yellow and R. Moyesi (red), are surrounded by
flaming Oriental poppies, iris, day lilies and peonies.*

Dooryard Garden in the Mormon Desert

Mrs. Elza H. Nixon HOLDEN, UTAH

Set in a beautiful Utah valley, the site of this garden would be semidesert if it were not for irrigation. But water—and twenty-five years' work —has converted it into as lush and colorful a flower garden as one would find in the well-watered East. But to achieve this the owner had to find what bulbs, perennials, annuals and shrubs would thrive in this rather special soil and climate.

Surprisingly enough, despite its exotic location, most of the garden plants are today the standard species of the country as a whole: the owner has merely eliminated those varieties which did not prove satisfactory. Thus, spring bloom comes from crocus, narcissus, hyacinths and tulips. These are followed by the old stand-bys of the herbaceous border: hybrid Oriental poppies (these have proved especially successful), delphinium, hybrid lilies and day lilies. There is, in addition, a collection of some 250 varieties of hybrid roses.

Late summer and fall color comes first from annuals—asters, zinnias, marigolds, snapdragons. Hardy plants include tritoma, dahlia, hibiscus and chrysanthemum. Another flower with which the owner reports outstanding success for late summer and fall color is the gladiolus. She plants hundreds each year. In late autumn the roses, too, take a new lease on life. They are supplemented by chrysanthemums, dahlias and snapdragons.

93

The Art of the Formal Garden

Jules Reingold

HIGHLAND PARK, ILLINOIS

DESIGNED as an adjunct to a house in the traditional French style, this is an excellent example of the frankly architectural garden, European in inspiration. Here the garden is not an integral part of the living area but rather a foreground and vista, artificially fashioned in keeping with the house and enjoyed as it is glimpsed through a window or in the course of an occasional stroll.

The linear severity of the forms lends to the garden a quality of chaste sophistication, of restraint and formality. The material employed to execute it are box and other hedge plants amenable to rigorous shaping. So strict is the pruning that the lines of the hedges and the low borders of the beds are scarcely less sharp in outline than is the brick wall with its stone coping. Except for the graceful scrolls terminating the beds leading to the distant statue, and the circular fountain in which it stands, the only curved lines in the garden are provided by the moundlike boxwoods and the slightly concave terminals of the central hedges. The entire area, too, is paved with crushed stone, which sets off the shapes and color of the symmetrically arranged beds and adds to the general air of precision and balance.

A few flowering plants placed between the boxwoods in the long, scrolled beds, and others inside the brick wall adjoining the house, offer color relief. Massed shrubs and trees in the background also do much to soften the visual effect of the garden itself, for the many greens of mixed deciduous foliage offer exquisite variety of shade, tint and texture, especially in early spring and autumn. This variety is in marked contrast to the unchanging though rich, dark green of box and other broadleaved evergreen hedge plants and ground covers. Nothing could be more effective as a foil for the strictly architectural design.

In this garden without flowers, the whole emphasis is on design. A few dwarf fruits may show their heads above clipped hedges, but the strictly formal, geometrical pattern is worked out in sheared box in panels and scrolls, with manicured specimens as accent points and ivy for carpeting.

Taming a View

Mr. and Mrs. Walter F. Isaacs
BELLEVUE, WASHINGTON

Good architectural and landscape design can often unlock the apparently insoluble problems raised by a difficult site. In this case, the site was a hilltop with a magnificent view of the mountains near Seattle. But this view had one shortcoming: it was to the west, and from that direction came hot summer sun and strong winter winds. The problem therefore was how to take advantage of the view and yet have garden areas suitable for outdoor living. The solution was to wrap a "U"-shaped house around a south-facing patio, creating a sunny, wind-free garden. But most of the principal rooms also overlook the mountain view to the west; and along this side of the house a partially shaded paved terrace was created for use when the weather permits. Also along this western side lies a handsome informal

A magnificent view of the mountains can be enjoyed from this paved and latticed terrace (above). The plot plan (below) shows how the house has been organized to afford a wide choice of exposures to sun, wind and view. Outside the kitchen is a herb garden (below).

PHOTOS BY DEARBORN-MASSAR

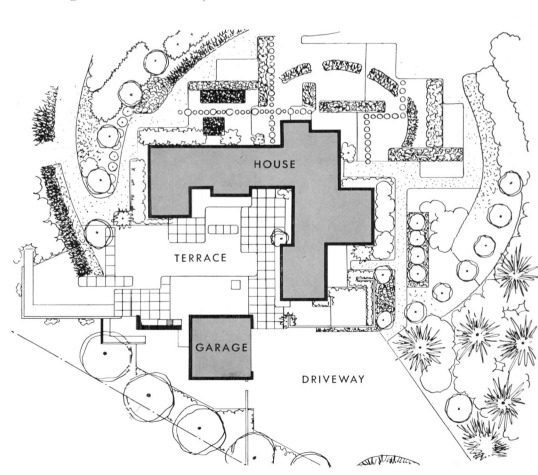

HOUSE

TERRACE

GARAGE

DRIVEWAY

planting of iris and native plant materials. This is kept fairly low so as not to interrupt the long view of the valley and mountains beyond.

Three criteria governed the design of the Isaacs gardens: ease of maintenance; year-round attractiveness; and the use of as much indigenous planting as possible. In the Pacific Northwest, the last

Above: *A big, old-fashioned cutting garden has been laid out along the west side of the Isaacs' house. Boasting a fine iris collection as well as perennials and herbs, the planting has been kept low to avoid blocking the view of the mountains.*

Left: *The house is wrapped around this south-facing patio to trap the sun and avoid the wind. Here the layout is basically architectural, with plant material used only for accent. Various paved areas offer a choice of sun or shade.*

Below: *This combination hall and conservatory, with its glass wall and skylight, overlooks the cutting garden and a view of the mountains. It is planted with tropical specimens that require year-round protection.*

two goals are readily attainable. The region has the most genuinely temperate climate in North America, with relatively cool summers and warm winters and plenty of rainfall the year round. For this reason it has a vast number of evergreen plants which, together with the lawns, are green throughout the year. The Isaacs garden uses many of these: mahonia, salal, currant, huckleberry, firs, dogwood, and so forth, and they have been used with imagination and taste.

96

PHOTOS BY DEARBORN-MASSAR

House on a Patterned Platform

Dr. and Mrs. Robert L. Worthington
BELLEVUE, WASHINGTON

CONTEMPORARY garden design, like that of the Renaissance, frequently makes a wide use of geometrical pattern. But today the pattern is usually asymmetrical as against the rigid axial symmetry of the Renaissance. This tendency is handsomely demonstrated in this new garden in the Northwest. Here a modern house is placed on a platform of interlocking walls, terraces, pools and planting areas. There is a close relation between indoors and out; and the garden is calculated to provide a wide choice of intimate views. This relationship, moreover, is preserved at night, since the garden has its own built-in system of lighting.

The main horticultural emphasis here is on spring bloom and rhododendrons, both of which are easy to achieve in the mild, moist climate of the Pacific Northwest. But the owners also wanted a garden that would be beautiful around the year—an especially important consideration where the house sits right in the garden and where so many walls are glass. As the pictures on this and the next page show, this has been delightfully accomplished with relatively simple and quite permanent materials.

This garden, conceived as a platform for a contemporary house, is laid out on a rectilinear grid to which paving, planting areas, pool and fences all conform. This provides dramatic background for specimen plants.

PHOTOS BY DEARBORN-MASSAR

The broad terrace of the Worthington house is built of very simple materials—concrete, wood, stone and gravel—handled with taste and imagination. Large paved areas are dictated by the climate, with its heavy rainfall and cool summers. Plants are hardy and mostly evergreen. The entire terrace area can be illuminated at night.

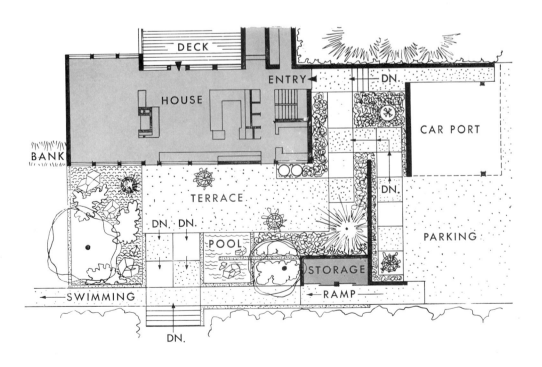

Walled Garden

in the Northwest

Mr. and Mrs. Ralph Nicholson

SEATTLE, WASHINGTON

WHERE the house is close to the street, as it is here, a "front yard" is worse than useless. It provides no outlook from the house itself; and it violates fundamental concepts of the privacy of family life. Here the problem has been neatly solved by placing a high, cedar board fence along the entire narrow street-front. This enclosure creates a little walled garden onto which the living room doors can open with security. Heavily planted with permanent materials—rhododendron, cut-leaf maple, bamboo, wisteria and conifers—the garden today gives an impression of being far larger than it actually is. Access to it is through solid double gates, painted after the fashion of Northwest Indian art. The path leads directly to the front door through a bower of foliage and is partially screened from the tiny garden alongside.

Placement of the little walled garden between the house and the street gives the living room a measure of privacy and quiet which is impossible with the conventional open front yard. Heavy shrubbery borders use cut-leaf maples, bamboo, rhododendron and conifers.

PHOTOS BY DEARBORN-MASSAR

Two views along the entrance path —one looking up toward the street from the front door (far left); the other, from the street, through wooden gates painted in Northwest Indian style, down to the front door. Heavy planting (left) screens walk from garden proper.

In contrast to the formal garden on page 94, color has here been employed to the full. Petunias provide red, pink and white; marigolds, yellow and orange; sweet alyssum, violet; lobelia, blue; dianthus, white, and so forth.

Tapestry for an Outdoor Room

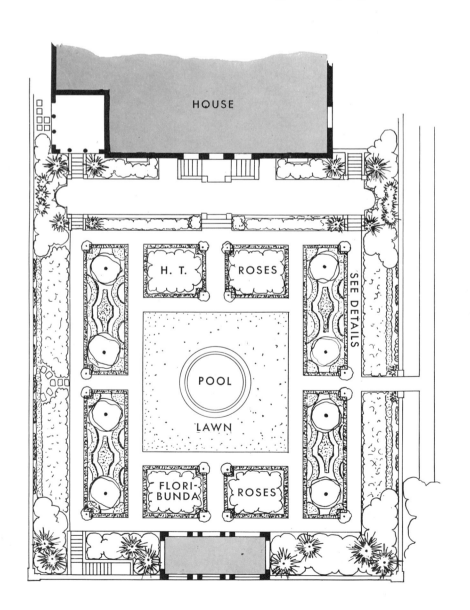

Richard Dwight Merrill

SEATTLE, WASHINGTON

Though the rather cool formality of the Merrill house is not typical of the Pacific Northwest, it is so firmly seated in its impeccable garden as to present a most persuasive example of its type. As a matter of fact, the cool moist climate of the area is what makes possible this type of garden, just as a similar climate favors the Luxembourg gardens in Paris of which it is so reminiscent. For formal designs of this sort place an extraordinary emphasis upon perfect maintenance; and hot, dry weather is the mortal enemy of perfect lawns and massed plantings of annuals such as this garden depends upon. Here the results are stunning: the sheet of emerald lawn, the controlled polychromy of the massed bloom, the frame of the clipped boxwood hedges—all combine to form a sort of living tapestry unrolled before the windows of the house.

Plant material has been selected with meticulous care to achieve the effect desired. No stress is placed upon specimen plants or perennials. It is a midsummer garden, planned to be at its peak during July and August. The annuals used are selected first for height (preferably only six to eight inches tall, and not exceeding eighteen), and second for color, so that, seen from even a slight distance, they give the general effect of a smooth carpet of blended colors, edged with boxwood green. These beds form a border for a panel of smooth green turf at the center of which is a severe, circular pool. Four small rectangular rose beds are lo-

cated at the corners of the turf panel, and the walks are surfaced with crushed granite. The vista from the house across the rose plots and the pool is terminated by a sizeable pergola flanked by a variety of evergreens, holly and a number of flowering shrubs.

Another interesting aspect of this garden is a collection of century-old espaliered fruit trees brought from Belgium in 1919 and displayed in the Pacific Exposition. These are trained against solid walls that flank the garden on either side. Still another rare feature is very old oleanders grown in large wooden tubs.

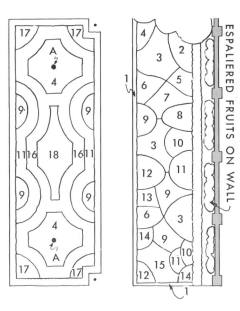

1 Lobelia Cambridge Blue
2 Snapdragon Swingtime
3 Verbena (white)
4 Alyssum Violet Queen
5 Ageratum Blue Perfection
6 Snapdragon Magic Carpet
7 Phlox drummondi (apricot)
8 Godetia (mixed double)
9 Marigold Yellow Pygmy
10 Petunia (pink)
11 Ageratum Blue Bedder
12 Alyssum Violet Queen
13 Phlox drummondi Chamois
14 Alyssum (white)
15 Phlox drummondi (apricot)
16 Alyssum Carpet of Snow
17 Mignonette Reseda
18 Verbena (salmon)
A Fruit trees—Apricot, Apple,
    Pear, Plum

Garden
in the Sky

Mr. and Mrs. Frank Greene
SAUSALITO, CALIFORNIA

Very often a highly desirable building site will have no place at all for a garden in the conventional sense. Problems of slope, view, or access will make it either impractical or impossibly expensive. Such was the case here. The site commanded a spectacular view of the Bay near San Francisco. But its slope was very steep and access was from the rear or landward side. To provide a solid earth terrace outside the living room, which was naturally placed to take full advantage of the view, was out of the question. The architects decided to build instead a large stilted wooden deck.

The result is astonishingly "garden like," despite the fact that the plant material is restricted to half a dozen potted plants—dwarfed pines and cut-leaf Japanese maples. This effect is partly the result of the material out of which the terrace is built (redwood and bamboo) and partly of the clever way in which it "borrows" the handsome foliage of its neighbors. To make the most of the view, the combination balustrade and bench is kept low and open. Only the sides of the terrace have high bamboo screens. These exclude neighboring structures on the one hand, and give the terrace visual privacy on the other. Slotted wood floors permit rapid drainage and prevent decay.

The two views on this page give a clear picture of the site problem: how to create a garden off the living room when it is far below street level on one side (left) *and yet far above the ground on the other* (above). *The solution arrived at was the handsome terrace shown on the facing page.*

Just how little plant material is needed to create a successful garden is
apparent in these two views of this terrace. Half a dozen dwarfed pines and
cut-leaf maples, all potted, do the job—though of course the design
does make good use of the handsome trees in the adjacent lots. Actually,
with a panoramic view of such dimensions as this any fussy detail
on the terrace would have seemed merely trivial. The checkerboard
decking is slotted for easy drainage and sweeping. For privacy, both
ends of the terrace are effectively closed off with bamboo screens.

PHOTOS BY MORLEY BAER

A Perennial Freshness

Mr. and Mrs. Raymond Haven Thayer
SAN RAFAEL, CALIFORNIA

Behind this grape-shaded terrace is a steep bank handled with characteristic California aplomb. It is densely planted in hardy materials which stabilize the soil and provide year-round, low-maintenance color.

THIS California garden has the kind of genial informality which only taste, time and good gardening practice can produce. Although it was begun over forty years ago by the present owners, it is still in a process of growth and modification. Hence it has many separate and distinct features, of which the arbor and rock garden shown here are only two. Other features include a large terrace off the living room, an outdoor fireplace, and a deck built over the creek that runs through the property. The garden is its owners' hobby and, as they put it, "grew through the pleasure of working out a garden of balanced beauty, in which there would be color and interest whatever the season of the year."

A steeply sloping site dictated its informal development and, over the years, the garden has assumed the form of a series of tilted rockeries laced through with a network of gently sloping paths from which they can be viewed.

The changes in level in this hillside garden are designed to make ascent and descent as easy and pleasant as possible. The broad shallow steps are constructed of creosoted railway ties backed up with crushed stone. The walls on either side are laid up without mortar and planted with a wide range of small-scale plants that need this kind of display to be properly appreciated.

PHOTOS BY PHIL PALMER: MONKMEYER

Designed by the landscape architect for himself, this rich and varied garden on a number of levels has been developed over a period of years on a slope that originally had no natural features of any sort.

Landscape on Five Levels

Herman E. Hein

MILL VALLEY, CALIFORNIA

DEVELOPED over a ten-year period by a landscape architect for his own home, this Marin County garden represents an interesting exploitation of its site. Built on a clear slope, sunny and wind-free but with no pre-existing features of interest, it has been developed in a series of five levels. These are all integrated into one design when viewed from the house and are lighted so that the view is, when desired, available at night. Since the climate permits year-round outdoor living, the garden is planted for year-round effect. This is mostly accomplished with trees and shrubs selected for the texture and color of their foliage. There is a wide range of flowering plants, including pool and rock-garden materials, but these are subordinated in the overall design. Like all professional gardeners, the owner has designed his landscape for maximum effectiveness with a minimum of upkeep. By heavy planting at the property line he has won a sense of privacy and seclusion without in any way impairing the atmosphere of spaciousness within the garden itself.

105

Although located on a modest suburban plot, this terrace combines spaciousness and privacy. Most of the trees which screen the end of the lawn, for example, are "borrowed" from neighboring property; while the wood fencing screens off the service yard and the neighbors beyond. Planting is simple, though the climate permits a range from the Juniperus Pfitzeriana *in the foreground to the* fatsia *against the fence.*

Garden on a Knoll

Mrs. Rebecca Wood Esherick

KENTFIELD, CALIFORNIA

Typical of current West Coast practice, this northern California house and garden is designed as an organic whole. There is, in fact, no garden in the conventional sense and scarcely any visual division between inside and out—an approach especially suitable to mild climates, where outdoor living is possible around the year. But instead of turning inward around a central court,

this house is placed in the middle of its land and faces outward. This setting raised problems of privacy and its opposite, outlook, and these the landscape architect has solved with great skill.

The land, to begin with, was a gentle knoll centered on a magnificent white oak. The house was located alongside this old tree and a system of paved and grassed terraces, all on one smooth level,

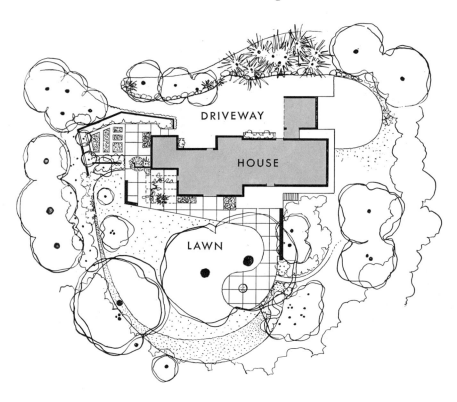

The terrace as seen from the rear of the lawn. The pergola, an extension of the roof framing, will ultimately be covered by the grapevines.

These two views show how the big, glass-walled living room has been organically united with the landscaping around it. Everything is direct and simple: the concrete paving, for example, is at the same level as the lawn to make mowing easier. There are no intricate details or finicky plants to complicate the maintenance.

was laid out to connect it to the house. Some earth fill was moved in to raise the lowest edges of the property. These areas were then heavily planted with shrubs and trees, which, together with existing trees beyond, now form a solid screen around the periphery of the plot. Thus the house today has the peace and privacy of a woodland park.

The simplicity with which the whole scheme has been developed has two important aspects. On the one hand, simple, flowing forms and uniform grades make a small tract appear larger than it is. On the other hand, they reduce both construction costs and maintenance problems. The terraces, for instance, are paved in ordinary concrete, their

surfaces brushed while still wet to expose the pebbles on top. The result is a textured surface, glare-free and non-slip. With this paving set at the same level as the lawn, the mower can be run right across both surfaces, thus eliminating much expensive trimming and edging.

From a functional standpoint, this layout is also effective for a family with growing children. There is little that children at play can damage with toys or games and a great deal of dry footing for use in damp weather. By the same token, these generous terrace areas are ideal for adult entertaining such as barbecue suppers around the grill under the oak tree.

For a family with growing children a whole series of landscape problems is neatly solved in this design—level lawns for games, paving for bicycles, a big brazier under the oak tree for barbecue suppers.

PHOTOS BY ERNEST BRAUN

provided in this house. It is sheltered on all sides by a system of deep overhangs and treillages. But he has gone further: he has set the house in the center of a man-made oasis. With water, fertile soil and desert sun, his plant material has achieved a jungle lushness (even such unlikely plants as bananas flourish here). This not only creates a green and glareless cushion for the house but acts as a soothing foreground for the desert views beyond.

Water from the surrounding hillsides, trapped during the rainy season, is stored in a series of concrete reservoirs. These the architect has brilliantly organized into a series of ornamental pools which girdle the house like a necklace. They form, in effect, a moat, and bridges lead across them to the oasis proper. In addition to irrigation, these pools have several functions. Visually, they form the outer boundary of the developed area: beyond them lies the untouched desert. They also act as an effective barrier to desert fauna—snakes, mice, scorpions, spiders and the like.

Plant materials are heterogeneous. Iris is used in large masses of solid color, interplanted with ivy and geranium, which is, of course, hardy and ever-blooming in this climate. Both cultivated and indigenous annuals are used for added color.

PLANT LIST

ORNAMENTAL SHRUBS
Abelia (pink)
Cotoneaster Harroviana (for drive screen)
Elaeagnus (for porch screen)
Lantana camara (for front terrace)
Myrtus compacta (for hedge to guest house
    and pool-edge groups)
Pittosporum tawhiwhi (for background planting)
Pittosporum tobira
Veronica
Viburnum
Oleander (or Nerium)
Feijoa sellowiana (pineapple guava)
Juniperus pfitzeriana
Plumbago capensis
Hibiscus
Juniper
Arborvitae

NATIVE SHRUBS
Ceanothus
Toyon
Giant Buckwheat
Sage
Rhus
Blackthorn

ORNAMENTAL TREES
White-flowering peach (for spring reflection
    in pool)
Acacia (three kinds with different blooming
    dates)
She-oak (Casuarina stricta)
Silk oak (Grevillea robusta)
Chinese paper tree (Tetrapanax papyriferum)
Loquat (Eriobotrya)
Queen palm (Arecastrum romanzoffianum)
Eucalyptus (four kinds)
California Pepper (Schinus molle)
Magnolia grandiflora
Parkinsonia
Poinsettia

SHADE TREES
California live oak
California pepper

Chinese elm (Ulmus parvifolia)
Carob
Camphor
Pine

POOL EDGES AND WATER PLANTING
Cattails
Agapantha lilies
Umbrella palm
Louisiana iris
Water hyacinths
Lotus
Water lilies
Creeping Cotoneaster
Reeds

VINES, WALL COVERS AND GROUND COVERS
Wisteria
Cup of gold (Solandra guttata)
Bignonia
Variegated ivy
Bougainvillea
Australian pea vine (Dolichos lihnosus)
Ficus pumila
English ivy
Dichondra

MISCELLANEOUS
Cacti
Succulents
Bush roses
Climbing roses (to cover banks)
Geraniums (on slope between house and guest house)
Aralia
* Iris
Day lilies (hemerocallis)
Bulbs
Cannas
Calla lilies
Dwarf ginger
Bananas
Philodendron pertusum

* Mrs. Moore breeds iris as a hobby. The entire promontory beyond the guest house is given over to her own hybrids.

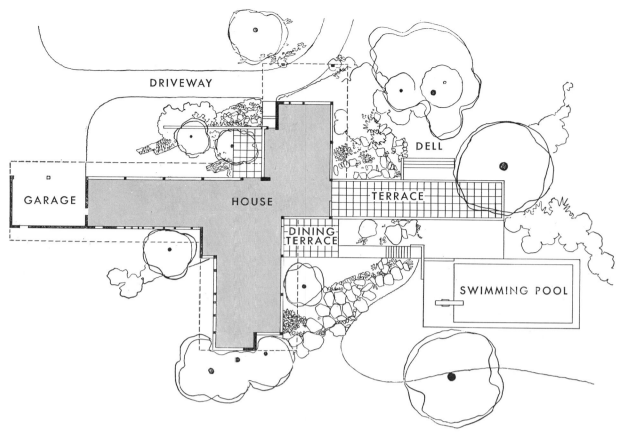

Cactus, Palms and Succulents

Mr. and Mrs. Warren D. Tremaine

SANTA BARBARA, CALIFORNIA

A detail of the rock garden surrounding the main living terrace. The contrast between its rich textures and exotic color and the view beyond is most effective.

JULIUS SHULMAN

THIS house is located in still another type of California climate, where intense sunshine and high temperatures are modified by the cool air, rain and fogs of the Pacific. One of the truly characteristic landscapes of this area is the meadow of native grasses studded with clumps of ancient live oaks. And it is in just such a setting that the Tremaine house is located. In their natural state, these meadows are green and flower-studded only in the spring, after the winter rains; later they turn a champagne-colored tint. But the air is dry enough for cacti and succulents to flourish; and warm enough for palms and orange trees. Thus an immensely wide range of plants is available in the region.

In this estate the landscape architect has wisely confined himself to two main elements: parklike areas of lawn and live oaks; and a spectacular rock garden of succulents. The latter has been skillfully

111

The unusual climate of the southern California coast makes possible
this juxtaposition of two quite different kinds of flora. It is warm and
dry enough for cacti and succulents (above). Yet the seasonal rains
provide enough moisture for live oaks and natural meadows (below), and
the latter can be converted into year-round lawns by means of irrigation.

Oriental Terrace
in the
Hawaiian Hills

The Honorable Mrs. Joseph R. Farrington
HONOLULU, HAWAII

This man-made platform, commanding a spectacular panoramic view, observes all the basic rules of such a feature: it is simple in form, level in grade, and enclosed to provide for the sense as well as the fact of security.

CLOSER to the Equator than even the southern-most tip of the United States, the Hawaiian Islands lie in a tropical zone. Unlike the continental tropics, however, this region never gets very hot; thanks to their position in the Pacific, the Islands have temperatures which—day and night, winter and summer—seldom fluctuate more than 5 degrees up or down from 75°F. In addition, of course, they have a generous rainfall, evenly spread around the year. These factors combine to make gardening in Hawaii a very different affair from what it is on the mainland.

In addition to exotic materials, both native and imported, Hawaiian gardens show a strong Orien-

The rocks are molded in a variety of mosses which thrive in the moist air. The velvety "lawn" is dichondra.

PHOTOS BY WERNER STOY: CAMERA HAWAII

In these views of the house and gardens the influence of the Spanish American tradition is everywhere evident. The brick-paved *allée* of olive trees and trimmed ivy ground cover captures the quiet and shade of old walks.

Here the clipped, squared-off beds outside the deep loggias of the house echo the geometric quality of the older style.

In the Tradition of Old Spain

Mrs. Archibald B. Young

PASADENA, CALIFORNIA

THIS is a fairly old Southern California garden, designed rather carefully in the idiom that the Spanish *conquistadores* brought to this part of the state. That it still seems so successful is a tribute to the basic logic and common sense of those early settlers. The long *allées* of silvery green olive trees, the use of water in movement, the firm but quiet linearity of its beds and paths—all of these are the marks of the great tradition which the Spanish inherited from the Moors. Though more formal and elaborate than present taste allows or current budgets can afford, the formula is still an admirable one for hot, dry climates.

PHOTOS BY FRED R. DAPPRICH

Garden on a Beach

Mr. and Mrs. Charles O. Martin
APTOS, CALIFORNIA

RONDAL PARTRIDGE

The Martin house has an unobstructed view of the ocean from its courtyard, despite the fact that, like most beach houses, it is built on a narrow lot. The view of the house from the bluff behind it (below) shows how its U-shaped plan and high redwood fences screen house and garden from neighbors.

Before the summer is over, a special kind of neglect overtakes most seaside houses: debris in the sand, sand in the house, dying shrubbery, and dead pot plants and pealing paint. To avoid this condition, beach houses and landscaping need to be designed to meet the special conditions of beach life. Oddly enough, they seldom are.

A beach that is lived on all summer does need to be brought under control but conventional elements like lawns and flagstone terraces generally do not answer the purpose. This house on the Pacific near San Francisco shows a really wise approach. Its small outdoor space is completely developed into a "garden," almost the entire area being covered with a slatted wood deck! The deck is made of redwood, which resists decay, and it is slatted to permit easy sweeping of tracked or wind-blown sand and to guarantee quick run-off of rain water. It is stilted high enough off the beach itself to provide space for the swept-off sand. And it is spacious enough to permit quite large groups of people to stand, sit or lounge in comfort.

At the same time, the basic pattern and texture of this decking has been used by the landscape architect to create a landscape of genuine beauty. The checkerboard pattern is interrupted by the free-form curves of raised planting beds and a little enclosed beach of sand for wind-free sunbathing. The major planting is of hardy materials with predominantly gray foliage; for example, ice plant (*mesambryanthemum*), a succulent ground cover, hardy in this climate, with handsome, spiky, gray-green foliage and masses of brilliant flowers in the spring. The garden is enclosed by wood fencing, also built of redwood, which gives it privacy from neighbors and protection from winds and sand.

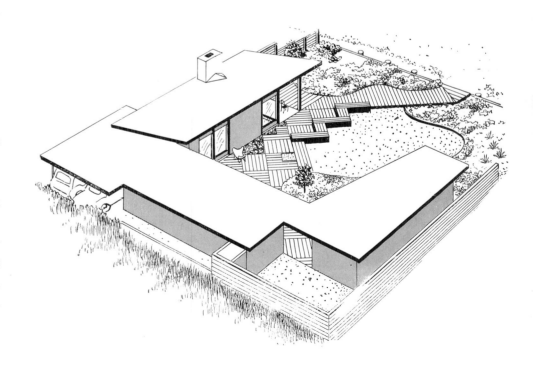

Beauty and utility are joined in the Martin beach garden, seen here from the living room windows. The lines of beds and boardwalks make a pleasant foreground to the ocean view; and such features as the enclosed beach for sunbathing and the slotted wood decking of walks and terrace make for easy upkeep and tidy appearance.

Swimming Pool to Match a Landscape

Mr. and Mrs. Dewey Donnell
SONOMA, CALIFORNIA

The cabana of the Donnell house, seen here from the pool terrace, is generously scaled for entertaining. Its sliding glass walls and big fireplace make it suitable for evening or cool weather parties.

120

A SWIMMING pool may be a source of great pleasure but it is ordinarily not an object of great beauty. Its size, depth, equipment and—until recently—blunt rectangular shape have confronted designers with serious esthetic problems. The solution, especially in colder climates where the pool was empty nine months out of twelve, was to tuck it somewhere out of sight. But the treatment is now changing, especially in warmer sections of the country, and the pool is often the central feature of the landscaping. This new pool in Sonoma shows the direction of the change.

In designing this pool-terrace-cabana combination, the landscape architect, Thomas Church, took his cue from the natural landscape. The site was a magnificent hillside location overlooking the broad sweep of the San Francisco Bay. The shore line at this point displays a series of smooth meandering curves on the flat valley floor. And the architect has echoed these curves in his design, using them to define not only the pool but the terrace, lawn and planting beds as well. Gone are all the usual marks of a swimming pool. The boxy shape is replaced by a free-form bowl and is centered by an island of abstract sculpture which echoes the boulders in the landscape. Pump and filtration equipment is concealed below terrace level.

By such means, the designer achieves a swimming pool which is as delightful to look at as to be in. An increasing number of people are finding that the same design principles work even in colder climates. The sloping walls of such pools allow them to remain filled all winter (the expansion of freezing water pushes the ice upward instead of outward, thereby eliminating the danger of cracking).

If this pool fits beautifully into its setting, it is because the landscape architect has carefully studied the magnificent view beyond it. The smooth, flowing lines of pool and terrace are taken directly from the valley below, with its curving shore line and softly molded hills. The handsome trees are native live oak.

PHOTOS BY RONDAL PARTRIDGE

Design for Desert Living

Mr. and Mrs. William Perlberg

PALM SPRINGS, CALIFORNIA

PALM SPRINGS, in the Southern California desert, is a winter resort area with a superb climate in the winter. This house is designed to take maximum advantage of this fact. Small but luxurious, it is wrapped around a patio, but the design problem was complicated by the fact that this fairly small area had to contain a large swimming pool which would also be handsome to look at.

The patio is all developed on a single plane: the floor of the house flows right throught the glass walls to become the floor of the porches, the walks and lawn of the garden: even the water in the pool is only an inch or two below this. Such a device minimizes the size and importance of the pool itself, reducing it visually to a turquoise shape in the pattern of the patio. Ladder and diving board are kept light and low, offering a minimum of disturbance to the composition. The lawn areas, while small, are very important in the design.

The whole complex is adroitly planned. Wide continuous porches give welcome protection to the glass areas as well as shade to the terrace (the palms, for all their exotic shape, give only token shade). And the rear wall of the garden, high enough for privacy, is low enough to frame a superb view of the mountains beyond.

The desert blooms in the well-watered patio of this winter house in Palm Springs. A good-sized swimming pool has been adroitly fitted into a small area and wide overhangs give shade from the desert sun.

JULIUS SHULMAN

This terrace, opening directly off the living room onto a spectacular ocean view, would not be practicable without the wind screen of clear glass around it which cuts off the sharp ocean breezes. Since the terrace is well off the ground, all plant material is potted, and flowering plants are replaced for continuous bloom.

MORLEY BAER (COURTESY OF LANE PUBLISHING CO.)

Outlook on the Pacific

Mr. and Mrs. Leslie Emery
CARMEL, CALIFORNIA

IT MIGHT be thought that a house overlooking Carmel Bay had beauty enough in its outlook, but the garden created for this one is not only lovely in itself but frames the view deftly. It forms a link with the bay so that there is no visual break from living room to beach. And all this has been achieved simply by placing the living room on the second floor and by means of a wide deck outside. Strong prevailing northwest winds are modified by the tall glass windbreak, as is shown in the foreground of the accompanying photograph.

Color is maintained throughout the year by the use of plants in large boxes and in pots, the latter subject to change at will. In the boxes grow such plants as *Coprosma baueri*, topped at eight feet, to serve as a screen for privacy, and *Choisya ternata* (Mexican Orange tree), kept trimmed to two feet. Trailing ivy covers the boxes. In the pots are grown such flowers as daffodils and other bulbs, primroses for spring, tuberous begonias for summer, succulents for winter, azaleas and cyclamen for Christmas. Driftwood arrangements play a part in the decor, harmonizing with the general atmosphere of the house and its environment.

About the grounds, the basic planting is largely of evergreens that get along with a minimum of care, despite the effects of strong winds and salt spray.

123

Flowering Roof Deck

Mr. and Mrs. Harold S. Simon

SAN FRANCISCO, CALIFORNIA

*From this breeze-swept rooftop garden one gets
a wide view, across the wharves, of San Francisco Bay.*

THIS site presented a double-barreled problem: first, to get plants to grow in the blazing sun on a rooftop; next, to have them low enough so that they would not interfere with the off-view of an open seascape.

The solution was found in selecting such low-growing, heat-resistant plants as *Alyssum saxatile citrinum, Festuca glauca,* artemesia, sedums and Irish moss, and such dwarf shrubs as Purple-leaf Plum, Acuba and Mugho Pine. These were planted in deep flats as well as in tubs. The spaces in between were topped with pebbles and small stones to give a desert-land effect in harmony with the plant material.

Near the entrance, where greater height was desirable in the plant material, camellias, fatshederas, aralias, azaleas and aucubas were massed for year-round greenery and seasonal color.

*The alyssum, artemesia, sedums, Irish moss
and* Festuca glauca *used here can stand the
sun and do not obstruct the view.*

PHOTOS BY ERNEST BRAUN

New Face for an Old Land

Mr. and Mrs. Alexander Girard

SANTA FE, NEW MEXICO

IN THE beautiful yet harsh countryside around Santa Fe, conventional gardens or grounds are out of the question. Only the hardy desert plants can live without protection from the hot sun, freezing nights, drying winds and blowing dust of

native building of the area—curiously "modern" in feeling. Thus Mr. Girard, who is himself a distinguished modern designer, was able to develop house and garden in the contemporary idiom. The entire garden area is laid out in a

PHOTOS BY CHARLES EAMES

The problems of this desert garden, similar to those of the roof deck on the preceding page, were solved in much the same way. The patio area, laid out in squares, is set out with such tough planting materials as alyssum, cacti, sedums and varieties of saxifrages.

the desert. Because of these conditions, even the smallest section of lush and flowering landscape becomes immensely valuable. Hence the traditional patio is the best answer to the needs of both plants and man.

Newcomers to Santa Fe, the Girards were nevertheless well aware of this when they bought an old adobe house and remodeled it. The house itself was unpretentious architecturally, more Indian than Spanish in design and—like all the

checkerboard pattern. The dividing strips are wood: some of the squares are paved, others are planted. The result is a pleasing design, of interesting texture and color.

A wide, shady porch off the living room is much used in warm weather; and the patio, spread out below, offers a pleasant foreground to the view beyond its walls. The patio is fully illuminated at night, with floodlights hidden in the eaves. Thus the striking pattern outside the living area can be

125

CHARLES EAMES

In addition to the patio shown on page 125 there is a raised area that is protected from the desert sun and allows somewhat less hardy plants, such as dwarf evergreens, small shrubs, herbs and potted plants, to be grown. Color—which most of the plants in this region lack during much of the year— is provided by furniture and accessories.

enjoyed both night and day.

Flowers that bloom in late spring and early summer do best in the Santa Fe climate and were therefore selected for color. Cacti, sedums and dwarf shrubs carry on for the rest of the year, with potted plants used around the porch. The results are most satisfactory, involving a minimum of maintenance and yielding a maximum of pleasure.

In the Foothills of the Sierra Madre

Mr. and Mrs. Floyd Mueller

PASADENA, CALIFORNIA

THIS house and garden, planned as a unit by the owner, is perched on rough ground high in the foothills of the Sierra Madre. The living room of the house forms a bridge across an arroyo or small gully running through the property. The informal garden which surrounds the house follows no conventional design. It is planned simply as a foreground to the view of the arroyo and the hills beyond—a view visible from every room in the house through wall-to-wall, glazed sliding doors.

Because of its altitude the site is considerably cooler throughout the year than most of the surrounding terrain. Occasionally the temperature falls below freezing, and therefore only plants that can withstand a light freeze are employed. All native plants growing on the land—such as sage,

126

yucca, "sticky monkey," wild gooseberry—were left where they grew or moved to new locations.

Such plant material as has been added was selected on the basis of its capacity to harmonize with existing plants, its ease of maintenance, and its resistance to light frosts. Of flowering plants, only spring- or autumn-blooming perennials have been used, and no annuals. Watering is done almost entirely by three "rain-bird" sprinklers, which cover most of the garden. Maintenance is kept to a minimum, and yet the garden—which was begun in 1948—continues to grow more beautiful year by year. Some of the plants have grown surprisingly; the fatsias, for example, have attained almost the stature of trees.

The plant material used includes the following:

Trees: Native sycamores; native live oaks; *Ulmus sempervirens* (Evergreen Elm); *Liquidambar styraciflua; Ginkgo biloba.*

Shrubs: *Fatsia papyrifera* (ricepaper tree); *Fatsia japonica;* acanthus; *Fatshedera Lizei;* oleanders; azaleas; camellias; hydrangeas.

Flowers: Daffodils, iris, day lilies; *Primula poyanthus;* saxifrages; violets; chrysanthemums.

Ground Covers: Ivies, *Ajuga reptans,* campanulas and ferns.

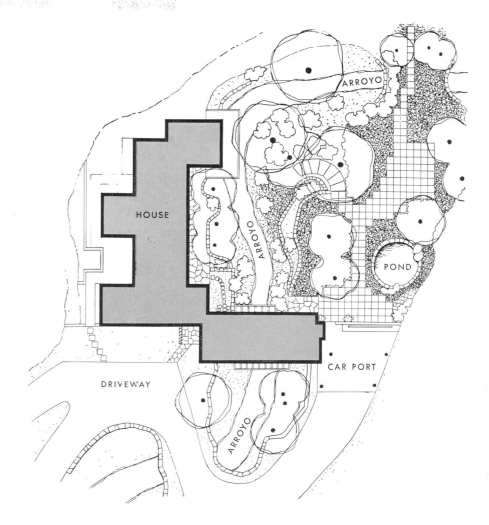

A beautiful "view" garden, this forms a frontispiece to the distant hills beyond. The planting around the house is intimate and informal, including much plant material not ordinarily grown in this region: for example, a ginkgo tree, several varieties of fatsia and liquidambars. Only perennials and hardy bulbs such as daffodils give color. Great care was taken to conserve the Live Oaks, Evergreen Elms, sycamores and similar native material.

PHOTOS BY JULIUS SHULMAN

Echoes
of
Spanish
Colonial

Mr. and Mrs. Everett De Golyer

DALLAS, TEXAS

*The loggia (A on the accompanying plan)
with its tiled floor and wide, sprung arches of
solid masonry recreates the traditional Spanish
colonial atmosphere and strikes the keynote
for this charming estate. The massive pottery,
plants in pots, and decorated wrought-iron
stands underscore this effect.*

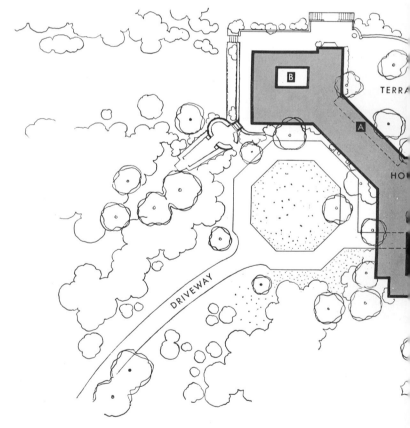

*Typically Spanish Colonial, too, is the patio
(B on plan) with its planting of semitropical
material, including palms, bamboo, acacias,
caladiums and bromeliads, and its winding
path decorated with a design in colored
pebbles and terminating in a massive arch.*

This semitropical garden has been skillfully developed to take full advantage of views across White Rock Lake, a large body of water on which the property faces. The landscape architects achieved this by arranging a series of gardens in a natural, flowing succession, each providing at least one advantageous view of the water.

Although constructed only about a decade ago, the walls and arches of masonry, the paved terraces and floors, the tiled roofs and semitropical vegetation, all suggest the early Spanish influence. The garden, however, is open and "outward looking" in the contemporary manner, making a happy combination of the old and the new. Bloom is continuous through most of the year, with abundant winter greenery and berried shrubs to maintain interest during the cold months.

The use of plants that are indigenous to the locality or thrive in the climate, and are planted in naturalistic patterns, makes for easy maintenance.

Much of the charm of this garden results from the surprise vistas that greet the eye along its paths.

Across a sun- and shadow-dappled lawn area is this view (D on plan) *down the long vista of the magnolia mall leading to the fountain.*

In this respect the landscaping differs from traditional Spanish Colonial with its concentration of planting immediately around the residence, but the divergence is so skillful that the traditional feeling is retained.

The place is approached along a curving, heavily wooded drive terminating in an octagonal court and the entrance to the residence. From the loggia at the rear of the residence there is a panoramic view of the lake across the "great terrace." The terrace is flanked on one side by the patio, with a path of colored pebbles in a distinctive design, and on the other with an expanse of lawn leading to a magnolia mall terminated by a fountain. From the mall, paths lead to the flower garden—connected also to the great terrace by a redbud allée—and to the rose garden.

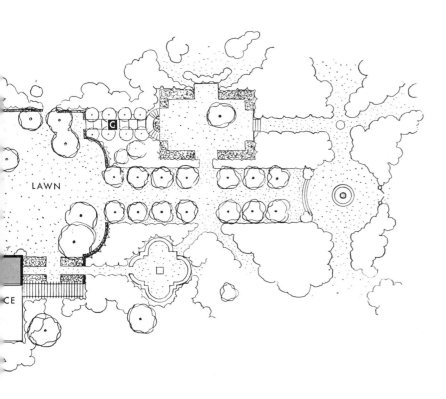

LAWN

CE

A somewhat different note is struck by the redbud allée (C on plan) *with its series of wide grass panels and cut stone steps, flanked by ivy-carpeted slopes, descending to the flower garden beyond. From the flower garden there is another wide view of the lake, framed by shrubbery and trees.*

foreground of still, black water—dyed a clear but brilliant black from the bark of the cypress.

An enduring beauty: Middleton Gardens

Of all the great historic gardens of America, none has had a more magnificent beginning, a more tragic period of destruction and neglect, or a more successful restoration than Middleton, at Charleston. Its renovator, J. J. Pringle Smith, is a direct descendant of its original owner and designer, Henry Middleton, president of the First Continental Congress and one of the first and most energetic leaders in the struggle for independence.

As it is displayed to thousands of visitors each year, Middleton Gardens is today perhaps the best-preserved remnant of the most ambitious formal garden in pre-Revolutionary America. The setting for a very extensive plantation house, long since destroyed, the gardens far surpass, in scale and richness, those of contemporaneous estates like Mt. Vernon or Westover. For Middleton was approached by a true water-gate which gave onto a vast system of patterned pools and cascading terraces. These led up to the platform on which the house stood. Originally, the planting must have been rigidly formal. Much of it has disappeared but the owners have wisely not tried to re-create it in all its intricate detail. The fascinating result is the sort of composition that only time can produce: magnificent specimen plants casually placed in a still-formal pattern of beds and walks.

The original gardens—now greatly extended with informal, azalea-lined paths—was conceived and executed by Henry Middleton. It was begun in 1741 with the purpose of giving the New World a garden that could rival any in the Old, plus a profusion of bloom impossible there. Much of the original growth was preserved—in fact two of the original great live oaks are still extant. The first camellias ever brought to the Colonies, four in number, were procured in 1787 from the French botanist André Michaux; and three of them are still alive! Today, the gardens boast one of the most famous collections of camellias in the world, thousands of plants in over three hundred varieties. Several pages would be required to list even the more important species now growing in Middleton.

Azaleas on an old plantation: Cypress Gardens

The second of the great swamp gardens at Charleston—Cypress—occupies the site of Dean Hall, one of the old rice plantations on the Cooper River. The lake around which the garden is organized is a natural one of fresh water, used in plantation days for irrigation of the rice paddies. The gardens themselves, however, are completely modern, having been begun some thirty years ago by the father of Benjamin R. Kittredge, Jr., the present owner. They are completely informal and, in fact, began almost accidentally—the owner having been struck by the beauty of an old azalea reflected in the swamp, which he saw while he was duck shooting. He decided to clear some of the banks and

plant azaleas and spring bulbs along them. The results were so spectacular that the garden was continuously extended, islands were landscaped, bridges built and thousands of azaleas planted.

For all its air of naturalness, Cypress has an extremely sound basic scheme. It is, first of all, a water garden whose main effects are designed to be seen from the water (and eighty percent of its visitors do view it from rowboats). At the same time, it has great horticultural interest in both native and cultivated plantings; and the paths permit a leisurely study of this aspect. Native growth

The gardens at Bellingrath in Mobile
are at once more formally organized and
horticulturally more complex than most of the
older gardens. The estate was until recently
a year-round private residence; hence twelve
solid months of bloom, rather than a short
spring season, was demanded. Although
it has many architectural features, such as
those shown here, the subtropical woodland
was left largely undisturbed. The result
is a garden of extraordinary botanical
interest, with a contrast between
meticulous formality and authentic wildness
that is unique.

is carefully preserved so that the entire 250-acre tract is, in effect, a wildflower and bird sanctuary.

Unlike some of the other gardens, Cypress has been developed for spring bloom exclusively (January through April), with emphasis on azaleas. Of these, in addition to *Indica* and *Kurume,* there are Ghent Hybrids and other types that elsewhere are not grown outside hothouses. There are also quantities of May-blooming gardenias.

Year-round bloom on the Gulf: Bellingrath Gardens

Bellingrath Gardens, like Cypress, is modern—begun in 1928 by the late Mr. and Mrs. Walter Bellingrath along the shore of one of the arms of Mobile Bay. It is like the other gardens of the area in its general outlines but differs in several important respects. Since it was begun as a garden for a private house, it is rather tightly organized around the house and much of it is quite formal in design. And since the residence was a year-round one, the planting scheme is aimed at year-round color. For the latter reason, the plant material is immensely more varied than in the other gardens—azaleas, gardenias and camellias being only the nucleus, so to speak, of the scheme. There is a great range of such summer-flowering shrubs as crepe myrtle, hibiscus and althea. A wide use is made of annuals and perennials for hot weather color. And, for the cooler months from Thanksgiving to Easter, thousands of pot-grown plants are produced: amaryllis, poinsettia, chrysanthemums, cineraria, calceolaria, fuchsia as well as such foliage plants as dracaena and croton. There is even a rock garden planted with African violets.

Though only a part of the Bellingrath blooming pattern, the azaleas are by no means unimportant: the gardens boast over a quarter of a million plants in five classes—*Indica, Kurume, macrantha, Belgian* and *Rutherfordiana*—and all colors. In addition, there is a fine collection of native azaleas (deciduous) in white, pink, yellow, cream and orange. These latter are naturalized in the woodlands.

More than 2,000 *Camellia Japonica* and *sasanqua* also bloom at Bellingrath, in hundreds of distinct varieties and all forms: single, semidouble, formal-double, rose-formed, loose-peony and full-

This deeply shaded flagstone terrace with its free-form pool and charming garden house adjoins the extensive woodland garden. Within, a bar, a cantilevered fireplace and dining facilities make it an ideal place for recreation. The flat roof has a wide overhang, and sliding metal screens can be opened to give direct access to the woodland area with its waterfall and shaded, winding paths.

Intimacy and Spaciousness

Mr. and Mrs. R. Vance Norfleet

MEMPHIS, TENNESSEE

ALTHOUGH this is not a small garden, it was designed to be, and is, a very intimate one. The owners are ardent gardeners; they also enjoy entertaining in an informal manner but on a generous scale. In the development of both house and grounds they therefore sought a combination of indoor and outdoor living, around the year and by day or night.

To attain these ends the orginal residence, quite conventional in style, was redesigned and the surrounding garden was screened off by a natural wooded area and by planting. This assures privacy

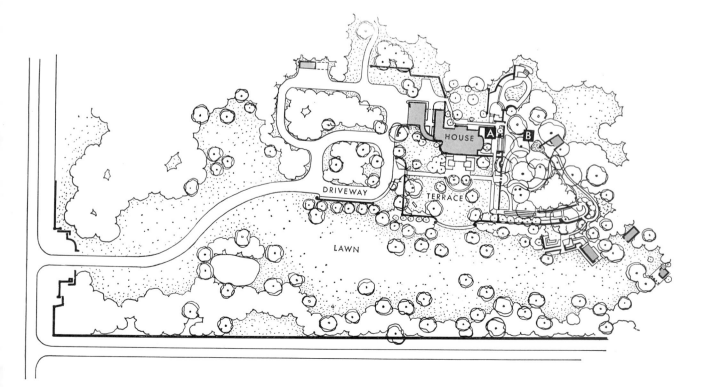

without the effect of being shut in. The component parts of the garden are connected to form a series of terraces, gardens and lawns—constructed, where possible, on different levels—thereby adding visual interest and increasing the apparent size of the whole garden area.

The entrance is designed to give the visitor a feeling of entering a garden rather than approaching a house. The service entrance is on another road, and completely hidden. The side of the garage flanking the entrance is treated as a tall garden wall and is decorated with vines and espaliered fruits.

The paved west terrace is semicircular in form, with table-height walls, overlooking a corresponding semicircular lawn area.

The south terrace and the living room are connected by glass doors and form a single indoor-outdoor unit. On the terrace a long, narrow lily pool extends along the base of the enclosing wall, beyond which lies the woodland garden. An outdoor breakfast-room terrace that opens off the dining room leads onto lawn areas.

A woodland garden, with a series of paths that are made gay in spring with native wildflowers supplemented by other suitable plant material, can be seen from the several gardens above it. The swimming pool is fed by water coming to it from a series of rills and cascades, the water being re-circulated by a pump in the garden house.

The work center of the garden, a very complete and practical unit, consists of a potting house, with space for tools and materials, and a slat-house which connects with a small greenhouse.

Among the plants featured in this garden are:

Trees: mimosa; Red Cedar; Sweet Gum; magnolia in variety; Black Gum; Royal Paulownia; American Linden; American Elm; dogwood; Purple-leaf Plum; Chaste Tree.

Evergreen, broadleaf shrubs: Abelia; Kurume Azaleas in variety; boxwood; camellias in variety; euonymus in variety; ilex (holly) in variety; Florida Jasmine; Cherry Laurel; nandina; photinia.

Deciduous shrubs: calycanthus (sweetshrub); Witch Hazel; Winter Jasmine; Beautybush; viburnum in variety.

Espaliered fruits and vines: dwarf fruits, and pyracantha and photinia in espaliered form. Vines: akebia; bittersweet, trumpet-creeper, wisteria, euonymus, creeping-fig.

The living room opens directly onto this flagged south terrace. The long, narrow lily pool on the right with the box hedge and low, stepped-back wall beyond increases the apparent width of the terrace. Abelia grows on the inside of the iron railing, and dwarf ivy on the near side. Potted plants are employed to give color on the terrace itself. Surrounding trees include hawthorn, crab apple, Saucer Magnolia and Chaste Tree.

PHOTOS BY CLARENCE JOHN LAUGHLIN

Ivied Seclusion

Mrs. George Weeks Hale
NASHVILLE, TENNESSEE

I N contrast to the Howe garden shown on the two preceding pages, the one displayed here was deliberately planned to provide maximum seclusion. This has been attained by the use of high walls, tall evergreens and screening vines. The overall effect is that of an old European garden that successfully closes out the clamor and disturbance of the surrounding world.

The garden was designed and its construction supervised in the late 1920's and early 1930's by the owner. The site is in a suburban development of the Belle Mead Estate, famous for the breeding of race horses. The climate is not a propitious one, the temperature ranging from above a hundred degrees in summer to an occasional ten or more below in winter, with prolonged droughts. The

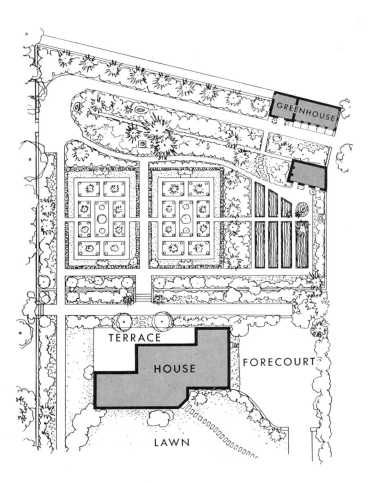

The effect achieved here is that of complete seclusion. With paved brick paths and iron gates enclosed by high walls festooned with ivy, it suggests an ancient monastery.

limestone soil has made the growing of ericas and broadleaved evergreens a difficult matter, but—despite some defeats—success with them has been achieved.

When the property was taken over, there was little existing plant material, since this section of the Belle Mead Estate had been a park through which some five hundred deer roamed at will. Still standing is a great oak where, in the early days of the present owners' occupancy, deer frequently came looking for the salt lick which formerly had been under it.

One of the heaviest tasks in constructing the garden was to gather the collection of sufficiently

140

The trees that contribute to the cloistered atmosphere here are coniferous evergreens, cedars and yews, together with broadleaved evergreens. The plant material has been purposely limited. Color is provided chiefly by lilacs, which are employed freely in the boundary planting, and, in spring, by many bulbs used in great variety in the borders.

weathered stones to build almost 1,000 feet of wall—of various heights—and two garden houses.

The boundary plantings are mostly of tall-flowering shrubs, with lilacs predominating, and a variety of broadleaved evergreens. Box and ivy are everywhere. At one time the place was reputed to possess the most extensive collection of ivies in this country—over one hundred different varieties. A severe ice storm, however, took a heavy toll of these. In the various borders around the garden are planted a profusion of daffodils and other bulbs in great variety.

Terraces and Patios

Terraces such as those shown in these pages are a basic part of the modern American house. Yet the terrace itself is anything but a modern invention—it is, in fact, one of the oldest elements in Western garden design. Those at Versailles are merely the most breath-taking in scope and splendor. Actually, every house of any pretensions in Western Europe and England boasted a terrace, and they were always valued for their recreational possibilities. (Old prints of palaces show the terraces full of courtiers "taking a turn" in the sunshine.) But the basic function of these Renaissance terraces was more to display the house than to please its inhabitants. They were designed much more to be seen than to be used.

We are beginning to learn that a well-planned terrace serves as an actual extension of the living area of the house. With a little common sense applied to their orientation and exposure, we can make them cool and shady in summer, sunny and windless in winter. Thus the amount of time that one can be comfortable out of doors can be measurably increased, even in northern latitudes. And, with the use of ever bigger windows and whole walls of glass, these terraces can be planned as visual extensions of the indoors, to be enjoyed no matter what the weather.

The two terraces shown here have totally differ-

Since the Longs' new house near Seattle is two stories high on the lake side and the living room is thus on the second floor, the upper terrace is built partly as a wooden deck and partly on solid fill.

ent forms springing from different purposes. The one on this page, owned by Mr. and Mrs. Joseph L. Long, Jr., surrounds a new house on the shores of a lake near Seattle. The house is two stories high, with the living area on the second floor. Here a wooden deck, slotted for drainage, has been built around the living room to provide lounging areas at that level and a commanding view of the lake beyond. The function of the other terrace (facing page), owned by Mr. and Mrs. Webb Moffett, is different. Here the site is constricted and without a view. Rather than use the limited space available off the living area for a lawn or a garden—either of which would be pleasant to look at but of scant use for outdoor living—the designers have wisely

This view of the terrace shows how securely it "ties the house down" and relates the living room to the grounds. Interior angle, where heavy traffic passes, is paved in concrete; remainder is in grass and at the same level for easy lawn mowing.

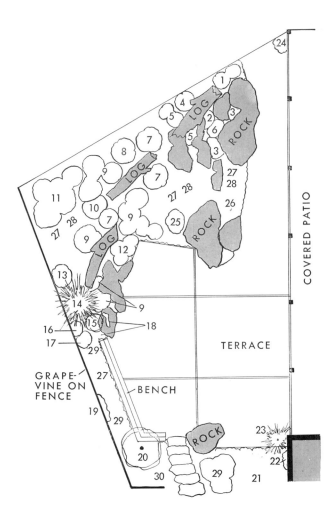

1   *Rhododendron racemosum*
2   *Rhododendron ponticum*
3   *Azalea ledifolia grandiflora*
4   *Skimmia (White-berried)*
5   *Pieris japonica*
6   *Pieris formosa*
7   *Rhododendron sutchuenense*
8   *Rhododendron (Beauty of Littleworth)*
9   *Azalea mollis*
10 *Rhododendron loders*
11 *Rhododendron discolor*
12 *Viburnum davidi*
13 *Photinia glabra*
14 *Pinus thunbergi*
15 *Cornus florida*
16 *Rhododendron (Souvenir of W. C. Slocock)*
17 *Rhododendron (Carita)*
18 *Azalea rosaflora*
19 *Rosa (Mermaid)*
20 *Prunus (Whitcomb Cherry)*
21 *Erica*
22 *Clematis armandi*
23 *Pinus contorta*
24 *Fatshedera lizei (vine)*
25 *Sarcococca hookeriana*
26 *Cyclamen*
27 *Primula*
28 *Begonia tuberhybrida*
29 *Tulips (with Begonia tuberhybrida later)*
30 *Gladiolus tristis*

The lush rock garden which encloses the big paved terrace of the Moffett house in Seattle was originally a raw bank about ten feet high. With imported stones and weathered, driftwood logs, planting pockets were created and filled with topsoil. This new garden constitutes the "view" from all living areas.

The basic aim of this garden is a rich, year-round composition. Thus it includes pines, dogwoods and azaleas; rhododendrons of many varieties; Pieris japonica and formosa. There is a large collection of heathers; many spring-flowering bulbs; and primroses, hardy cyclamen and tuberous begonias.

chosen to make the whole area into a paved terrace. The rock garden along the back of this terrace serves to enclose it, giving a sense of privacy to the area and creating a view of year-round interest. The covered porch is an important auxiliary to the terrace since showers are frequent during warm weather in this region.

Above: *The modern patio of the Chinn house in San Francisco serves the same function and uses much the same materials as the old ones: only the forms and patterns are changed. A paving of integrally-colored concrete makes a charming abstract design that is colorful, trouble-free and child-proof. Planting is hardy and minimal.*

Left: *This 200-year-old patio, known in New Orleans as the Brulatour Courtyard, shows the classic Spanish-Arab conception. Basically an outdoor room furnished with a few plants, it is paved because of the heavy rainfall.*

Below: *An early nineteenth century patio, beautifully restored for Mrs. Frances Parkinson Keyes, reveals both French and American influence. The proportion of greenery to paving is higher and there is more emphasis on such flowering shrubs as crepe myrtle, pomegranate and roses.*

In California and Louisiana

THE TERM PATIO has of late been vulgarized to include any outdoor paved area. Originally— and properly—it defined an open courtyard, usually in the center of the house, like the Roman *atrium* or the Italian *cortile*. In this country, the patio was introduced by the Spanish, who used it wherever they went in the New World. It was then, as now, an excellent climate-control device, especially in subtropic areas. And this is why it has enjoyed such great popularity in recent years: people have discovered that it makes outdoor living possible, even in northern climates.

146

The patios shown on page 146 are both new and old. They happen to be located in areas where the Spanish first introduced the form two centuries ago—San Francisco, Los Angeles and New Orleans. Of course the modern patios show great differences in design and plant material from the old

The patio of the Beauregard House in New Orleans, now the home of the well-known writer, Mrs. Frances Parkinson Keyes, is a recent restoration of a garden which dates from the 1820's; similarly the patio of the Brulatour Courtyard is a restoration of the patio of the Brulatour Mansion,

JULIUS SHULMAN

Modern horticulture makes possible the luxurious rain-forest planting seen in the Hollywood patio of Burton Schutt. Royal palms, fatshedera, bananas and tree ferns—separated from the living room by only a sliding glass wall—lend an Oriental seclusion to a garden not far from a busy street.

ones. But basically they all have one quality in common—they extend the actual living space of the house beyond its walls. They also extend the time that one can comfortably spend out of doors by providing wind-free sun-traps in cool weather and shady, cool areas in hot weather.

built in 1816. The patio of A. B. Chinn's home in San Francisco is, on the other hand, a recent construction. At first glance, the two old gardens and the new one appear quite unlike; but the difference is more apparent than real. Both rely mainly on patterned beds and paving for effect. In

A small garden in Morristown, New Jersey, has here been reconstructed with taste and common sense. Instead of a lawn—difficult to maintain— the ground is surfaced with crushed stone. The curving flower beds are neatly edged in concrete blocks. Fence and furniture are in durable cypress. Evergreen planting is supplemented in summer by potted flowering plants.

both, plant material is subordinated to architectural elements, especially paving, which is essential for dry footing in such rainy climates. Precisely because it is sparse, the plant material gets added emphasis and drama. In the California patio (page 147), there is a more informal use of exotic growth; and the glass wall of the living room makes it an actual part of the interior. In all three cases, however, the effect is to weld house and garden into a single unit.

Transformed Back Yard

THE TERRACE of the B. F. Swain garden (above) in Morristown, N.J., illustrates what can be done in very limited space and for a small outlay. It represents the transformation of an unattractive back yard—which had as its "view" a still less attractive yard immediately adjoining it—into a se-

cluded spot that invites informal outdoor living.

The change was achieved by the owner, under the guidance of landscape architect Alice Dustan, with very inexpensive materials. The plain wooden fence was given character and interest by the simple expedient of staggering the boards instead of placing them edge to edge in the usual way. The gracefully curved retaining wall for the miniature raised flower and shrub border is constructed of ordinary cement blocks, and the area is floored with crushed stone. Table and benches, practical but of unusual design, fit perfectly into the overall picture.

The plant material, too, is inexpensive—azaleas, ilex, andromeda, hostas and several others for year-round beauty, and caladium, geraniums (in tubs) and a few plants in pots for summer color. That's all there is to it, and yet it makes a charming little garden.

148

Terrace in the Clouds

A GARDEN maintained on a city rooftop year after year with many permanent plants and trees is in its way a minor miracle. Such is the New York garden (below) of Mme. Helena Rubinstein.

And it is a real garden, not merely a conversation piece, as so many rooftop plantings are. A wide variety of plants and trees give a sequence of bloom throughout the season. Tulips and other colorful bulbs, azaleas and forsythia welcome the spring, and are followed by lilacs and espaliered fruit trees, including apple, peach and plum. Annuals and other later-blooming types continue to supply color through summer and autumn. Even a number of wildflowers find a place. The basic background material, which includes rhododendron and ivy, provides year-round greenery. A wishing well in one corner and a small herb plot in another not only add interest but enhance the illusion that this is a true down-to-earth garden.

Despite heat in summer, frequent biting winds in spring and fall, and such urban phenomena as smoke and smog, plants are maintained in good condition through constant and expert care and culture. Much of Mme. Rubinstein's extensive entertaining is done on the terrace, and there on hot summer evenings the freshness, fragrance and beauty of this exotic garden are most appreciated. Both the plantings and the furnishings have been

This penthouse terrace in midtown Manhattan is a true garden, not—as so often happens—merely a display of potted plants from the local florist. Such gardening represents a victory over many hazards—high winds, dust and soot—that the average gardener never meets.

149

kept simple to create an atmosphere of relaxation. On frequent occasions the garden is opened to the public for various charities and for visiting garden clubs.

Outdoor Dining Room

IN EFFECT the terrace of the Umberto Innocenti garden (below) is a sheltered but unwalled extra dining room; it has the specific function of allowing early spring and late autumn enjoyment of the garden on days when, without such a place, the family would be spending the time indoors. Its surrounding low, wide brick walls provide a safe foundation upon which to place flowering plants in low boxes or flower pots, and also a windbreak for taller ones placed on the floor.

The use of wrought-iron and glass all-weather terrace furniture minimizes maintenance. The slight elevation makes an ideal vantage point from which to view the panorama of the seasons, from the emergence of spring until the last leaves flutter down to blanket freezing soil.

Objective: Peace and Privacy

A MAXIMUM in the peace and privacy which an outdoor living room may offer has been achieved in the terrace of the Long Island home of the well-known landscape architect, Richard K. Webel.

This small dining terrace at the Innocenti home on Long Island is fitted into a sunny, sheltered corner of the house. It overlooks a lawn and border of specimen shrubbery worthy of the greatest of English estates (main treatment on pages 65–67).

These two views of the Webel garden (right and below) *on Long Island show a charming little design at its springtime best. Double-flowered tulips, azalea and* Magnolia stellata *will be followed by bedded annuals.*

Plants and flowers have been employed primarily as living furnishings and decorations. The harmonizing, graceful curves of the paved area, the unbroken turf terrace beyond it, and the surrounding wall which protects it, all combine to create an atmosphere of sheltered serenity.

Often in the planning of house and garden the opportunity for creating such a quiet retreat as this—separated from the more active play area and colorful but not visually peaceful flower borders and rose beds—is overlooked. Where such an area is provided, however, it is usually a source of great

satisfaction to its owners, and with the passing years becomes more and more effectively adapted to its original aim of peace and privacy.

Plants used in and around the shaded terrace shown above include hydrangeas, ivies, *Vinca minor*, with a perennial border at the foot of the surrounding wall in the foreground.

In a Tropical Frame

THE GARDEN AND PATIO of Mr. and Mrs. Robert Huntington in Palm Beach (over) is another in-

The peacock is an amusing bit of topiary work in clipped yew. Designed in a highly personal style by Richard Webel, well-known landscape architect, this garden shows that distinction is not dependent upon large size.

PHOTOS BY GOTTSCHO-SCHLEISNER

stance, like that of the Sharples garden on page 142, where native plant material in Florida has been handled in such a way as to create a really tropical atmosphere instead of the usual formalized pattern.

Here a cleared, sunny area is surrounded not by a formal, wall-like border, but by an irregular, continuous band of native plant material which makes the open area appear as though it had been wrested from an encircling jungle. The generous-sized ground-level patio, paved in simple rectangles, opens to a view so framed at sides, top, and bottom as to intensify this tropical atmosphere. A wall or a hedge at the edge of the patio would have lessened immeasurably the whole feeling of the scene. The contrast between the cool shade of the patio and the brilliant sunshine on the lawn beyond makes the dining area particularly inviting.

In a Genial Climate

JUDGING BY THE SALE of mowers, the lawn is the favorite garden feature of American home owners. More time and money is spent on its construction and care than on any other aspect of the landscape. Yet, for a variety of reasons, much of this effort is wasted. Sometimes the fault is that of geography—many areas of the country are too hot in summer or too cold in winter to permit a genuinely perennial evergreen lawn. Sometimes the fault is that of construction—poor soil, inferior seed, and so forth. Very often, the fault is simply that of design—the lawn is improperly placed or laid out with relation to the house or the rest of the grounds.

The lawn of the Austin Earl garden (facing) is a model of what most lawn-owners would like to achieve. It is located in central California, south of San Francisco, where the climate has only one deficiency—lack of sufficient rain during the dry season. This is corrected by a built-in sprinkling system. It has been beautifully constructed and superbly designed as an integral part of the living terrace of the house. Although actually not much larger than the average city lot, it is so skillfully laid out around two fine old oaks and so cleverly enclosed by an elliptical border that it gives the effect of a spacious English park. Thus the effort has been concentrated where it counts most—around the garden front of the house. Planting is simple but effective: the genial climate permits masses of geraniums, hydrangeas and tuberous begonias whose pastels are brilliantly displayed against the clipped emerald of the lawn itself.

This terrace on the Huntington estate in Palm Beach makes a point too often overlooked in that sunny region: the great importance of shade. Here, instead of the ubiquitous coconut palm, are native bays and magnolias combined with palmetto, ferns and mosses. The result is at once functional and exotic.

152

RONDAL PARTRIDGE

This superb lawn at the Earl place in central California, expertly constructed and maintained, has a velvety texture which is in stunning contrast to the beds of foaming pink hydrangeas and clipped ivy. Although actually not very extensive, its shape gives it a feeling of great spaciousness. The bed around the live oaks is planted with tuberous begonias.

Rock Gardens

THE ROCK GARDEN is a highly specialized form of ornamental horticulture. In general such gardens in America have been none too well designed. They had no place in the early European-inspired planting around Colonial homes in the South or in the monastery-type designs of the Southwest. As for northern Colonial home-builders, they were more concerned with getting rid of rocks than with utilizing them for decorative effects.

In Japan rocks and stones have for centuries been employed in the making of gardens, but in a manner quite different from that in any Occidental scheme of decorative planting. In Oriental landscaping, each stone is selected for its own beauty and symbolic meaning. Even their placement in relation to each other, and in fixed patterns, has par-

ticular significance, just as has each "line" in a traditional Japanese flower arrangement. In America only in comparatively recent landscape designs tailored to accompany decidedly modern architecture, and mostly in the West, has this Oriental approach to the use of rock occasionally manifested itself.

In England the Occidental, naturalistic type of rock gardening has long been employed and has reached the highest degree of excellence. There the use of dwarf, trailing evergreens and of dwarf flowering shrubs has been more general than in American rock gardens; such plantings are very helpful in achieving a truly naturalistic effect, but they require considerable time to develop full beauty and the quality of rugged individualism which best fits their surroundings.

153

These adjoining views of the Samuel C. Dretzin place in Chappaqua, New York, show how the dense deciduous woodland on the far side of the lake forms a magnificent natural backdrop for the rock plantings in the foreground. A native rhododendron at the extreme end of the left-hand view carries the eye down to the azaleas, phlox, myrtle, euonymus, and other ground covers.

English rock gardens have served as models for American landscape architects. The greatest impetus to this phase of gardening in America was given by the rock gardens staged in flower shows—and installed by private owners—by the English landscape architect Ralph Hancock during the late 1920's. Just prior to his displays there had been a period when rock gardens became a fad, and the American scene was affected with a rash of what became known as "peanut brittle rock gardening" —small, round boulders stuck in polka-dot fashion on sloping banks and interspersed with varicolored patches of creeping phlox, alyssum and candytuft. Not infrequently the stones themselves were painted, making the general effect even more artificial. Fortunately this craze waned almost as rapidly as it developed.

Today the rock garden, either by itself or combined with some water feature such as a pool or a small stream, offers the owner of a moderate-sized place an opportunity for a specialized, intimate type of gardening in which he can grow a collection of extremely interesting, diminutive plants

from many parts of the world. The rarity and difficult culture of many of these present a challenge and add a fillip for many keen gardeners.

Enchanted Landscape

ALTHOUGH AT FIRST GLANCE the landscape on these two pages seems to be largely an expanse of placid water, it is in reality a far-flung rock garden, with a series of large pools serving to reflect and enhance the beauty of trees, shrubs and rock plantings which surround them.

The entire property, owned by Samuel C. Dretzin of Chappaqua, N.Y., is an outstanding example of what may be done, even with a most unpromising and difficult site, by turning apparent obstacles into vantage points. Here, instead of employing extensive and expensive blasting and grading, the landscape architect modified the existing terrain as little as possible, utilized local plant materials and supplemented them with species and varieties such as rhododendron, hardy azaleas, and dwarf pines that would strike no jarring note in the

154

general natural effect. The construction of this garden was undertaken in the fall of 1948—considerably less than a decade before the accompanying photographs were taken.

A Rarity: The Tropical Rock Garden

Rock GARDENS are traditionally identified with Alpine plant materials but this is largely the result of the fact that in their present form they were developed in the cool climate of England. The English, in turn, had imported this type of garden from China and Japan, where much of the plant material had come from the Himalayas. But the origin is an accident of history: a rock garden could quite as easily be tropical as Alpine. This is convincingly demonstrated in the handsome rock garden at

A cabana perched on a rocky promontory on the far side of the water is surrounded by a profusion of spring rock garden flowers with azaleas blooming all around.

Bellingrath (below) on the Gulf Coast near Mobile.

From the standpoint of esthetics, the success of a rock garden depends much more upon the skill and taste with which it is constructed than upon the plant materials used. This is especially true when the garden is developed with imported stones rather than out of indigenous live rock and ledge. The Bellingrath garden is very successful in this respect. It is equally successful in its planting which, to northern visitors, is astonishing because the species range from dwarf Kurume azaleas to African violets! Since the gardens are open to the public around the year, bloom is desirable in all seasons. Hence quantities of seasonal material are raised elsewhere and moved into the rock garden for the blooming period. While most home owners are not able to do this type of gardening, it is a principle that could well be applied on a small scale to selected spots of special importance in the garden.

Rocks, Woodland and Meadow

A STRETCH OF ROUGH, rocky hillside, woodland and a meadow in a swampy valley were the raw materials available to the landscape architect who was asked to create for Leonard J. Buck of Far

In the famous Bellingrath Gardens, near Mobile, massed blossoms of large azaleas cascade over an outcropping of natural rock to meet such dwarf plantings as A. kurume, *heathers, ligustrums and* Buxus hanlandi. *Azaleas are massed in the foreground, and campanulas bloom freely to the right of the brick path. Northern visitors to these gardens are often amazed at the African violets grown in the open as rock plants.*

The landscapes on the estate of Leonard J. Buck (see also the following page) *in Far Hills, N.J., are works of consummate art in that they appear completely natural. Forest trees and shrubs, such as holly, laurel, blueberry and other natives, form a setting for rock gardens where rare alpines and all kinds of native material flourish side by side.*

Hills, N.J., "a landscape with a garden in the woods, with view panoramas and surprising vistas into varying and interesting plant colonies." The designer was Zenon Schreiber, who has won many gold medals for rock and garden displays.

While the terrain in general lent itself to such a development theme, a dense network of tree and shrub roots in a thick layer of loose traprock, with very little top soil, presented serious problems. By following existing contours and constructing strategic paths, a series of seven different rock gardens was evolved. From these and the paths which connect them, surprise vistas reveal open fields and shadow-patterned woodlands, some of which are shown on this and the next page.

In the selection of plant material the first consideration was suitability to location and existing conditions. Species native to eastern woodlands such as dogwood, laurel, blueberry, azaleas, rhododendron, pine and cedar were utilized to the fullest extent. Then intensive effort was made to acclimatize promising aliens. Here, naturally, some fail-

ures were experienced, but many have succeeded, thus adding greatly to the variety and interest of the whole planting. Alpines from western states and from Europe and the Orient—many of which, incidentally, are closely related—have proved to be a great asset. Among these are: *Azalea hakata shiro* (dwarf) and *Rhododendron williamsianum* and *obtusum* varieties; *Campanula coclearifolia* and *C. elatinus garganica;* Helianthemums Ben Nevis, *appendinum, nummularium* and *polyphyllum;* sempervivums in variety; potentillas *megalantha, verna nana* and *villosa;* geraniums *renardi, sanguineum prostratum* and *cinereum;* primulas *veris* and *P. sieboldi alba; Dianthus alpinum;* gentianas *acaulis* and *septemfida,* and saxifrages in variety.

As this garden is planned for year-round enjoyment, care has been exercised to provide maximum color and interest for each season. In spring there are azaleas, dogwood, genistas, blueberry, marsh marigolds, cypripediums, anemones, native columbine, trilliums, hepatica, bluets, wild geraniums, primulas, and saxifrages, to name but a few. Sum-

157

In this view of the natural woodland quality of the Buck estate, dogwood and other native trees and shrubs are visible above the vertical rock face. On the rock itself, dwarf iris promises future color. At its foot, native red columbine raises its red, starry blossoms among foam-flower and saxifrages. In the foreground, blue wood phlox, creeping phlox, yellow helianthemums and white anemones are combined with rare alpines from Europe and the Orient.

mer color is provided in part by rhododendrons, heathers, clethra, helianthemums, potentillas, gentians and sempervivums. In fall there are the red berries of dogwood, ilex and cotoneaster and the colored foliage of blueberry and other shrubs. Pines, junipers, heaths, brooms, laurel and rhododendron provide winter greenery.

For Color and Informality

DESIGNED WITH IMAGINATION and good taste, the rock garden, even on a small place, may be one of the most colorful and rewarding of all planted areas. None of the three presented on page 159 occupies a large space and yet in each a great variety of fascinating plants is grown. When a small pool, trickling stream or a miniature waterfall is combined with the rock work—as in most cases it can be—each will almost always enhance the other greatly.

By its very nature the rock garden is far removed from the rectangular lines and the symmetry of the formal garden. Where much of the overall landscape design must follow a somewhat conven-

Marsh marigolds are shown growing near the water, with ferns, anemones, trilliums, Geranium sanquineum alba, sempervivums and many other woodland rock plantings.

tional pattern, the rock garden, if it is not to be an obtrusive feature, must be given such a backdrop of trees and shrubs that it will blend into the surroundings without distinct lines of demarcation. By the same token the plant materials used in it should be such as seem naturally to associate themselves with rocks—trailing and semitrailing perennials, dwarf trees, shrubs and evergreens, and low-

Above: *Brilliant color is achieved in the rock and water garden of the Coopers in Brookline, Massachusetts, by accents of rosy-red azaleas, rose and pink* Lychnis alpina, Aubretia deltoides, Dianthus alpinus *and creeping phlox; by yellow* Alyssum saxatile citrinum *and pansies; and by white arabis,* Iberis Gibraltarica, *cerastium and* Phlox subulata. *Varied greens of summer-blooming species, including heathers, add to the overall effect.*

Left: *The wall garden of the Nixons of Mendenhall, Pennsylvania, has been planted in much the same way, with perhaps a little more reliance on lower-growing species.*

growing bulbs, especially species and species hybrids.

It will be noted, too, that in the three gardens illustrated, the stone used in each case is of one general type and so placed as to simulate a natural rock formation. This effect cannot be achieved if different types of rocks are employed in the same garden or if they are placed in anything approaching a systematic design.

Right: *At Newton Center, Massachusetts, Mrs. Frances Friedman has used late narcissus, tulips, myosotis and Siberian Wallflower among large boulders in a wide border on sloping land.*

Designs with Water

IN LANDSCAPE design the use of water in one way or another can be a most important factor. Like the rock garden, the water garden may be utilized as effectively on the small place as on the spreading acres of a large estate. Between the two, however, there is one very important difference, for water may be used with equal appropriateness in either the most formal or most informal kinds of landscaping, whereas rock gardening does not lend itself to use in formal designs. Examples of both types of water gardens are shown here.

A distinction must of course be made between water gardening in the more specific sense (i.e., the growing of aquatic plants) and the use of water as an element in garden design. The former is a special kind of gardening that employs water as a medium in which to grow plants; the latter is a matter of fitting water—a pool, a stream, a pond or a waterfall—into the general landscape scene. Sometimes, of course, these two uses are combined.

Where water is utilized as an important element in the landscape it may set the esthetic mood for the whole picture, ranging from the sunlit pond or sparkling stream to the somber, shaded pool. One of the simplest and most effective ways of using water is to let it serve as a mirror and thus emphasize whatever charm the surroundings may have. The mirror may be tiny, such as that in the Davison garden (page 162, bottom), or an extensive one such as in the Choate garden (page 165). A pool also has the magical power to capture the sky and bring it down to ground level to form a background of azure blue or fleeting clouds for flowers, trees or garden ornaments.

The charm of water used either within a garden or in a more extensive landscape will depend very largely upon the character of the plants that are grown adjacent to it. They should be those usually associated with water in nature, or those especially attractive in reflection, such as weeping willows, birches, both the upright and weeping form, ornamental cherries and crab apples, and—among smaller plants—rushes, mallows, Japanese iris and the like.

A common mistake where a pool, either large or small, is an element in the design is that of overplanting. Too many varieties of plants or those that eventually grow too tall will tend more or less to obliterate a pool or make it visible only from a second-story window. Much of the charm of the wide expanse of water in the Choate garden or the diminutive one in the Davison garden would have

Along the edges of this long, informally treated body of water, in the Charles W. Nichols garden, rocks have been well used to hold the banks and to harbor such plants as statice, water iris, decorative grasses and cerastium. The restraint in the planting allows emphasis where it belongs—on the water itself.

160

The wide pool, reflecting sky and tree forms, is planted only with Weeping Willows backed by pines and deciduous trees. The landscape has the dreamy quality of a Corot—appropriate setting for a French provincial home.

PHOTOS BY GUY CLARK JR.

been lost had not restraint in this respect been exercised.

For Distant Views

GARDENS IN THE formal style surround the French provincial residence of Mr. and Mrs. Charles W. Nichols of West Orange, New Jersey, with its tower and tiled roof, and blend house and grounds into a harmonious unit. The purpose of the informally treated water areas (above and on facing page) was to provide pleasing distant views from the house that would contribute even more to the general effect of a French country estate with outlying forest and farm areas.

Around the house, formal gardens with their many flower beds are relied upon to provide bold masses of color during spring, summer and fall; suitable evergreens form sturdy backgrounds and winter foliage patterns. Even though stimulating in their colorful beauty, the flower borders, edged with box and enclosing smooth *tapis vert* panels, create a contemplative atmosphere. Here the invitation is to simple solitary relaxation.

In developing this estate the landscape architect had to solve problems posed by soil, climate and topography, The establishment of desired grades involved heavy cuts, much earth-moving and the building of many walls, steps and slopes. The soil was a heavy, impervious clay, necessitating elaborate tile drainage systems. The selection of plant materials required a good deal of experimentation since in addition to soil that was recalcitrant, temperatures ranged during the development period from the high nineties during summer to as low as twenty-six degrees below zero in winter.

In contrast to the larger bodies of water shown on pages 142 and 154, the two on this and the facing page illustrate the magic that may be wrought by the inclusion of even the smallest of pools in an appropriate setting. It accomplishes two things; first it immediately creates a focal point in the picture, and secondly it gives it greater depth—a projected, third dimension. In addition, water always attracts birds, and so the element of movement is also added to the scene.

In Miniature

WHAT CAN BE DONE with water as well as rocks in a limited space is illustrated in the Frey garden (page 162, top) in Caldwell, New Jersey. There is a charm of the miniature in the little pool

The gemlike quality of Orian C. Frey's rock and water garden is created by the use of such plants as long-spurred aquilegia, trollius, violets, Cotoneaster horizontalis and umbrella plant. The selection and placement of rocks and flowers represents a masterly fusion of the natural and the designed.

and the streamlet edged with mossy rocks and set off by columbine, primulas, coral bells, ferns, succulents and similar rock garden plants. Above them, rhododendron and a variety of broadleaved evergreens reach toward the water, forming a backdrop of rich, glossy foliage.

Given a stream, moisture and shade, either natural or artificial, a rock garden such as this can be created even on a very small plot of land. Or it may form one of a series of foot-stopping, eye-filling details in a more extensive planting.

In the Davison garden in Oyster Bay, Long Island, care has been exercised not to overplant immediately around the pool, and low plants only —such as forget-me-nots, pansies and violas, grape hyacinths and doronicum—have been grouped in such a way as not to obscure the water from view.

The plants used in this garden include Clusiana tulips, primulas, arabis, *Alyssum saxatile* and English daisies, replaced in midsummer with tuberous

Blue myosotis, grape hyacinths, campanulas, yellow doronicum, wallflowers, and white and pink English daisies and arabis spread a wonderfully colorful scarf of spring flowers around a tiny pool in the Davison garden.

begonias and greenhouse foliage plants in pots. A fine flowering crab overhangs the little pool.

Design in Blue and Gold

A STRIKING use of water occurs in the Moore home (right and pages 108 to 110) California, where the pool comes up to the very wall of the house. The severity of the lines of house and pool are relieved by golden acacias, other flowering shrubs and aquatic plants set among natural rocks. At the far end a mass planting of calla lilies blooms outside the glass house wall. Beyond this, the pool provides a colorful foreground for the blue of the distant mountains and a mirror for the flower garden around it. Though the mountains are not actually reflected in the pool, the repetition of soft blue in the water and in the misty hills beyond gives unity to the whole.

As Motion and Music

IN THE HAWAIIAN GARDEN on page 164, water is almost literally brought into the house, as is sometimes done in Japan. A formal pool takes the place of a porch along one wall, and a rockbound stream, with a naturalistic planting along its edges, follows the contour of the wide curving steps leading up to the house. Here, instead of providing a tranquil reflecting mirror, water adds motion and musical sound to the scene. As a design, steps and stream seem to be flowing down the slope together in a twin rhythm that invites one to ascend and enjoy the shadowed coolness within doors.

As a Mirror

IN SHARP CONTRAST to the way water has been employed in the Hawaiian garden is its use in the formal gardens (page 165) of Miss Mabel Choate in Stockbridge, Mass. Here, instead of the movement and music of flashing miniature waterfalls are the placid surfaces of box-rimmed pools, arranged in a strictly Old World design of dignified formality. Without a ripple or even a lily-pad to break their glassy surfaces, they faithfully reflect

JULIUS SHULMAN

Moonstone blue sky, hills and a mirror pool frame this home in brilliant bands. Set around it in nearly tropical profusion are pittosporum, Pyracantha duvali, Viburnum carlesi, oleander and other flowering shrubs; Louisiana Iris, water lilies, lotus, water hyacinths, cattails. agapanthus and callas; such rock garden plants as succulents and cacti; and, just visible at the side of the house, a banana plant.

The home of Mrs. Katherine Johnson in Honolulu, this is an excellent example of the merging of house and grounds in design, choice of materials and atmosphere. The palms and all the tropical shrubs and flowers contribute to the unity of effect.

the classic architectural features and trimmed and tailored landscape plantings surrounding them.

It would be difficult to find more illuminating examples of the difference in spirit and atmosphere between the old, traditionally formal, and the new, completely informal approaches to landscaping than as exemplified by these two gardens. The Choate garden, although not directly connected to the house, invites one to stroll through it, possibly to sit down for a while and enjoy the quietude amid the trembling, translucent pools.

The Johnson garden (this page), on the contrary, is definitely *an extension of the house.* The pool adjoining the house wall, and the rock-edged stream with the broad steps descending alongside it have been carefully planned as an out-of-doors continuation of the residence. Visually there is no marked break between them, and it is difficult to determine where one ends and the other begins.

PHOTOS BY BEN PANG

An interesting use of water in a garden of strictly formal, old fashioned design is seen in this segment of the Choate estate (main treatment on pages 76–77). Here a combination of jet fountains and pools, edged with meticulously clipped dwarf box, provides an elaborate pattern against a background of vine-covered pillars.

ARTHUR C. HASKELL

Specialized Plantings

For one reason or another, on a large place or on a very small one, the owner frequently gets his greatest pleasure by concentrating on a garden devoted to one type or group of plants, or even to a single species. Sometimes such a garden is skillfully designed and presents a most attractive picture; in other cases the gardener's effort is concentrated wholly upon the culture of the selected plants, and these are grown to produce the finest specimens, the most complete "collection," or possibly new varieties. Everyone, for instance, is familiar with the dahlia or chrysanthemum fancier whose garden may be an unsightly miscellany of posts, sticks, or even dilapidated umbrellas, but who regularly wins the blue ribbons at his local flower show.

In the American scene the hobby or specialty garden decidedly has its place. Frequently the owners of such gardens are the moving spirits in the special plant societies which have contributed and are still contributing so much to the advancement of horticulture in the United States.

Sometimes the specialty garden is employed as a part of a general-purpose garden in order to create scaping the grounds of houses of Spanish or modern design in tropical and semitropical areas.

Unlike roses and other flowering plants favored by the gardeners in northern sections, the succulents require a minimum of attention and are drought-resistant to an almost unbelievable degree. Many of them have bloom of marvelous beauty, but their interesting growth patterns and the wide range of coloring to be found in their foliage are of even more importance in landscaping. (See illustration at bottom of preceding page and on pages 112 and 113.)

Annuals on Cape Cod

THE EARLY AMERICAN HOUSE that the Silas S. Clarks acquired a few years ago in Wellfleet on Cape Cod had nothing left in the way of a garden but a steep, sandy hillside overgrown with brush, scrub pines and locusts. The remains of some post-and-log terraces, a few iron-hardy yuccas and native cactus were all that suggested that the area had once been under cultivation.

The Clarks like color and realizing that annuals would give them the quickest results they concentrated on these. The effect achieved was remarkable, especially since, as in all locations near the sea, annuals here take on particularly brilliant coloring (below). Each winter the owners search seed lists from here and abroad for new varieties or species, and the garden has developed into a sort of living catalog of annuals, each kind being grown to remarkably fine quality. With the passing of time, bulbs for early spring bloom, masses of roses and perennials—especially chrysanthemums to stretch

In this split-level garden on Cape Cod, the Clarks have converted a sandy hillside into terraces of brilliant color, with annuals predominating. At extreme lower right appear the foliage of the Spanish Bayonet plant, Yucca filimentosa, *and the native, hardy cactus,* Opuntia compressa, *which in season show, respectively, towers of ivory-white bells and tropical-looking yellow saucers. The slopes are clothed with masses of petunias, zinnias, marigolds, alyssum, poppies, godetias, nemisias and such tender bulbs as gladiolus and dahlias. There are also large plantings of roses.*

F. F. ROCKWELL

The Oregon garden of Jan de Graaff, the world's leading hybridizer of new lilies, overlooks the Sandy River canyon. Many of his latest creations, planted in beds in and around a bricked terrace, create a breath-taking effect.

the color late into autumn—have been added. One shaded terrace is devoted to tuberous begonias, gloxinias and the like; but this garden is still primarily a wonderland of annuals.

Lilies in the Northwest

OVERLOOKING THE FIR-CLAD SLOPES of the scenic Sandy River gorge in Oregon, the sky-line garden belonging to the Jan de Graaffs has two special features—daffodils in spring and lilies in midsummer. This is not surprising, for the owner's business is the growing of bulbs, chiefly daffodils and lilies, for the gardens of America.

Gardens in which lilies are featured have, in the past, been few and far between, for the lily, although acknowledged as the queen of bulbous flowers, has been considered a bit on the difficult side, self-willed and somewhat unpredictable from the gardener's point of view. This view has been the result in part of the fact that the wild species of lilies, found in many different parts of the world, for centuries resisted hybridizers' attempts to get them to intermarry and thus produce horticultural types and varieties for use in the garden. Within the past two or three decades, however, this reluctance has been overcome, and the resulting

hybrids intercross readily, providing many new types more amenable to garden uses than their wild ancestors. As a result, lilies are more and more becoming a hobby flower.

Rivers of Iris

IRISES FROM EVERYWHERE, and from the earliest recorded ones, way back in the sixteenth century, down to the very latest introductions, all gathered in one place—this is the remarkable achievement of the Presbey Memorial Iris Gardens, Montclair, New Jersey, internationally recognized as one of the most complete collections of iris in the world (next page).

Equally remarkable is the fact that this project was begun as a community undertaking, with no special funds to finance it. The Garden Club of Montclair conceived the idea of starting such a garden and originally sponsored it, securing John Wister, noted authority on iris, to plan the landscaping. The town supplies the site, the manual labor, fertilizers, etc., required to maintain it. The Club provides the new plants to keep the garden up-to-date and a committee of some forty-five horticulturally-minded citizens does all the supervising, planning and marking; and provides guides during

GOTTSCHO-SCHLEISNER

Iris of all types and colors comprise the renowned Presbey Memorial Iris Gardens. Sponsored by the Garden Club of Montclair, it is one of the show gardens of New Jersey.

the flowering season for the thousands of visitors who come from far and near to admire or to study.

Where Garden Flowers Take to the Woods

THE MOST REMARKABLE FEATURE of the garden (below) of Mrs. Charles R. Walgreen in Illinois is that the owner has specialized in taking horticultural plant materials and treating them as wildflowers—a complete reversal of the usual procedure. Thousands of daffodils and tulips, hundreds of iris, hemerocallis, chrysanthemums, tree peonies and Christmas-roses have been planted in and along the edges of the forest of oaks, locusts, hickories, pines and hemlocks that surrounds the spacious lawn at Hazelwood, an estate overlooking the Rock River at Dixon, a hundred miles west of Chicago.

The purpose of developing this unusual type of landscaping was to provide masses of bloom for viewing and an inexhaustible supply for cutting from spring to autumn and even into the winter. Moreover, instead of concentrating on a few varieties of each species, as is generally the practice in naturalizing flowers, here each kind has been planted in wide variety; there are, for instance, over seventy varieties of hemerocallis.

Easy maintenance was also a prime consideration. The flowers selected were for the most part those capable, to a large degree, of taking care of themselves. Of all the bulbs used, the only ones that need to be taken up for the winter are dahlias and ismenes. Through the woods beyond the flower borders, furthermore, the slopes are covered with a wide assortment of wildflowers. They include such natives as bloodroot, anemones, wild

"Untaming the garden flowers" is the unusual theme of Mrs. Charles Walgreen's garden at Dixon, Illinois, where thousands of spring-flowering bulbs and summer- and autumn-flowering perennials have been naturalized in and along the forest's edge.

MYRTLE R. WALGREEN

170

The charm possible in a "wildflower preserve" is everywhere evident on the 65-acre estate in Woodbury, Connecticut, where Frank G. Shinn has assembled one of the most complete collections of eastern species of wildflowers.

ginger, mertensia, shooting star, Dutchman's breeches, squirrel corn, hepaticas and Jack-in-the-pulpit. These have been encouraged to grow, but receive no further attention.

Hazelwood quite naturally has become something of a mecca for the garden clubs of Illinois. The annual spring "garden walks" held here help raise funds for the Lincoln Memorial Garden at Springfield, which is a project of the Garden Club of Illinois.

Wildflowers by the Acre

"BEAUTY IS WHERE YOU FIND IT" is the theory upon which Frank G. Shinn has developed in Woodbury, Connecticut, one of the most extensive and best-known privately-owned wildflower preserves in America (above). He has carried on his work in the conviction that it is very much easier to encourage native plants to grow and increase in their natural habitats than it is to bring them into man-made gardens.

The scene of these endeavors has been a 65-acre farm, formerly the site of an old sawmill, with stream, waterfall and pools, which lent itself admirably to the purpose. By dint of ditching, draining and clearing some of the low, wet marshland was made suitable for moisture-loving species; and by continual thinning out of wooded areas, he has kept just the degree of openness which suits upland species. In addition to the native flora, which was unusually extensive, friends and visitors from all over the East have brought or sent the owner species or subspecies that were not already growing in his own or neighboring woods, fields and swamps. The list of wildflowers he now has growing in his series of gardens—which includes rock, swamp, meadow, woodland and pool—reads like the index to an encyclopedia of native Eastern flowers, shrubs and trees. And all of these gardens come as near to taking care of themselves as it is possible for any garden to do. In the owner's words, they require little or no more attention than that usually given a moderate-sized lawn and flower borders.

Index to Owners and Professional Landscape Architects and Designers

* Member of Garden Club of America

174

* Member of Garden Club of America

Set in 12-point Lino Fairfield
Designed by Andor Braun
Printed and bound by Kingsport Press, Inc., Kingsport, Tennessee
Color and monochrome engravings by Chanticleer Company, New York
PUBLISHED BY HARPER & BROTHERS, NEW YORK